Twayne's English Authors Series

Sylvia E. Bowman, *Editor*

INDIANA UNIVERSITY

Arthur Wing Pinero

 150

Arthur Wing Pinero

By WALTER LAZENBY

Eastern Illinois University

Twayne Publishers, Inc.   ::   New York

Preface

In *Arthur Wing Pinero* I have tried to introduce the reader to the fifty-seven works of a playwright who had a significant role in developing the modern English drama but whose reputation has been obscured by the more brilliant achievement of George Bernard Shaw. The fact that Pinero was not a Shaw does not warrant certain prevalent assumptions largely dismissing Pinero as an "archbishop of the obvious" and as "the Franz Liszt of the drama," and I have consequently tried to counter them with a fairer assessment.

Since few persons can be expected to remember Pinero's plays in their original performances; since they are infrequently revived (like many other good plays) and mostly out of print; and since even specialists in dramatic literature will probably not know more than two or three of them, I have analyzed them all. In commenting on them, I have tried to go beyond a bald summary and to focus on the playwright's selection and arrangement of events to tell stories from the stage, believing that the critic of dramatic literature must observe the peculiarities of dramatic form. The plays themselves are, after all, the most trustworthy evidence for a study like this one. I have treated them according to Pinero's advice in "The Theatre of the Seventies": ". . . in dealing with the stage you must judge an author's work in relation to the age in which he wrote, the obstacles he had to grapple with in the shape of ancient prejudices and seemingly impassable barriers. . . ."

Assuming that plays which share similar effects ought to be discussed together, but also wanting to emphasize Pinero's varied achievement, I have grouped the plays according to types. For chronological listing of the works, the reader may consult the bibliography, where dates of composition and publication are given. The dates which in the text follow play titles (in parentheses) are those of first performances.

To E. P. Dutton and Company, for permission to quote from Clayton Hamilton's *The Social Plays of Arthur Wing Pinero*, and to The University of Chicago Press, for permission to quote from Wilbur Dwight Dunkel's *Sir Arthur Pinero*, I express gratitude.

For assistance of various kinds, I am indebted to Patricia Davis, Don Bermon Bailey, Richard Fisher, Mrs. Vinita Davis, Ruth Gray, and the Graduate Council, all of North Texas State University; and to Anthony Cuccio, Jay Trost, Cathy-Lynn Jackson, Gary Forrester, and Dr. Robert F. White, of Eastern Illinois University. I gratefully acknowledge my heavy debt to my friend Dr. James M. Linebarger and to my wife, Sharon, for proofreading and editorial advice.

WALTER LAZENBY

Charleston, Illinois
January, 1972

Contents

Chronology

1855   Arthur Wing Pinero born May 24 to John Daniel and Lucy Daines Pinero, at 21 Dalby Terrace, Islington, London.

1865   Withdrawn from school to study law in his father's office.

1865–   Frequent theater-going; saw first performances of T. W.
1871   Robertson's "cup-and-saucer" plays.

1870–   Employed as assistant clerk to a solicitor; studied elocu-
1874   tion in evening classes at Birkbeck Institute; composed first plays; failed to get them performed.

1874   On father's death, abandoned legal career for acting.

1874–   Acted in stock companies at Edinburgh and Liverpool and,
1881   after 1876, at Henry Irving's (London) Lyceum.

1877   First performance of one of his plays, with Pinero in cast; resumed playwriting.

1879   Met actress Myra Holme.

1880   Production of his first hit, *The Money-Spinner*, in Manchester.

1881   Gained notice as emerging author with three London successes (*The Money-Spinner, Imprudence,* and *The Squire*); joined company at Haymarket Theatre.

1882   Retired from acting; his play *Girls and Boys* performed, with Myra Holme in lead role.

1883   Married Myra Holme.

1883–   Wrote seven full-length plays; produced six.
1884

1885–   Composed and produced popular farces for the Court
1893   Theatre and *Sweet Lavender,* his longest-running play, earning fame and fortune; these plays adapted on the Continent.

1885   First efforts as a director; record-breaking run of *The Magistrate* at Court Theatre; made his only trip to America.

1887   Wrote *The Profligate,* a landmark in development of the English problem play; elected to Garrick Club.

1889   *The Profligate* performed, but ending altered.

1891   *The Times,* first British play to be published under newly revised International Copyright agreement; copies sold on opening night.

1891–   Studied Continental masters; composed *The Second Mrs.*
1892   *Tanqueray.*

1893   *The Second Mrs. Tanqueray* acclaimed the best English play since Sheridan's *The School for Scandal;* Pinero's royalties thirty thousand pounds.

1898   Produced his best sentimental comedy, *Trelawney of the "Wells."*

1899   Produced his finest comedy of manners, *The Gay Lord Quex.*

1899–   Extensive but intermittent travel on the Continent.
1903

1906–   Produced three of his best plays at St. James's Theatre:
1909   *His House in Order* (1906), his greatest financial success; *The Thunderbolt* (1908); and *Mid-Channel* (1909).

1907   Recovered from illness; prolonged stay at Wiesbaden to recuperate.

1909   Knighted for his contribution to stage literature.

1912   *The "Mind the Paint" Girl* booed; his output and popularity declining.

1919   Death of Lady Pinero.

1928   Fiftieth anniversary of his debut as a playwright celebrated by Garrick Club.

1934   Died on November 23.

CHAPTER 1

Man of the Theater

ARTHUR WING PINERO early chose a lifework connected with the theater, and he eventually had three different careers in it, as an actor, a playwright, and a director. Born to well-to-do liberal-minded parents in 1855, he enjoyed the opportunity of attending the theater as a youngster. He was taken by his parents to a pantomime at the Grecian Theatre in the City Road "when he was a mere infant"; and he was later frequently given the price of a seat in the pit at Sadler's Wells, which was near his boyhood home in Northeast London.[1] In the years when he attended it, Sadler's Wells was probably the foremost theater in London, artistically, under the management of Samuel Phelps, who was known for his revivals of Shakespeare, his acting ability, and his high standards for production.[2] When Sadler's Wells began to decline, the stage-struck boy transferred his loyalty to the small Prince of Wales's Theatre under the management of Squire Bancroft and Marie Wilton (later Mrs. Bancroft), where T. W. Robertson's so-called cup-and-saucer drama first gained acceptance. Here he absorbed the artistic aims of Robertson's quiet plays and the lifelike Prince of Wales productions.[3]

At the age of ten, Pinero was taken out of the school in Exmouth Street, Clerkenwell, and placed in his father's law office to prepare for a legal career. Thereafter, his education, aside from legal studies, consisted of sporadic private tutoring, night classes at the Birkbeck Institute[4] (now part of the University of London), and a trip to France, probably before 1870.[5]

When John Pinero retired to a country estate near Greenwich in 1870, young Arthur independently found work in a library; but after a few months he resumed his study of the law, taking a place as clerk to a solicitor in Lincoln's Inn Fields, where he remained for nearly four years. Starting at one pound a week, he eventually rose to a salary of one pound ten shillings (about $7.50 then).

Because the family's finances were now in precarious state, he contributed most of his income to the common purse at home.[6]

In the nine years spent in lawyers' offices Pinero developed a loathing for the dryness of the law, yet eventually he profited from his sufferance of it. He learned the importance of details, partly from his father's occasional neglect of them.[7] He came to know lawyers' clients and their problems, especially those arising when restrictions are placed on the living by the dead. He became confirmed in a skeptical or at least disingenuous outlook on human nature. His experiences served him well as an objective writer of problem plays and more or less led to his dealing, in his mature plays, with well-to-do people whose lives have gone awry without their having made any serious missteps.

More important, the young clerk took respite from his dull routine in ways which nourished his imagination and his esthetic sense. He delighted in the study of elocution at night school and chose as his valedictory exercise recitations from the role of Hamlet. He attended the theater whenever he could, to worship his theatrical idols. Having learned that the most eminent men of the theater frequented the Garrick Club, he often ate his meager lunch hurriedly and during the rest of his lunch hour stationed himself across the street from the club in hopes of glimpsing one of his heroes.[8] And he wrote his first plays. Evidently a dream of success in the theater occupied his mind even in working hours, as his own testimony reveals:

The truth is I was stage-struck almost from my childhood, and while I was in Lincoln's Inn Fields I was often guilty of suborning my companion and, behind my employer's back composing dramas and sending them about to the various theatres. My manuscripts were always accompanied by a letter written, to impress the recipient, on my employer's note-paper, and I remember how discomfited I was on one occasion when inadvertently he opened a letter from a London manager addressed to myself, saying "Dear Sir, Your stuff is of no earthly use to me. For God's sake, fetch it away as soon as possible." [9]

Fortunately, he was not seriously discouraged by his discomfiture about the letter and by his rejections but persevered to gain, eventually, the right to enter the portals of the Garrick Club himself.

I *His Debut as an Actor*

Pinero took his first major step toward realizing his dream in 1874, after his father's death and the settling of his family's affairs. Free now to make his own decision about a career, he joined one of the last of the stock companies at the Edinburgh Theatre Royal as a "general utility" actor. During his apprenticeship there he had time to read plays, to study their construction, and to observe R. H. Wyndham's expert direction. Though the work was not especially challenging, requiring mostly changes of costume and seldom any speaking of lines, Pinero was very happy; and, in the final year of his life, he spoke nostalgically about his feeling of accomplishment and about the congeniality of his work.[10]

In scarcely two years the novice progressed from the provinces to the theatrical capital and with his acting attracted the attention of three important men of the theater. In 1875, after fire destroyed the Theatre Royal, Pinero had to seek actor's work elsewhere. With good recommendations from the Wyndhams, he went to Liverpool, where he gained the notice of Wilkie Collins. Through Collins, he obtained an introduction to R. C. Carton, manager of the Globe Theatre in London, who engaged Pinero to appear in the London première of Collins's *Miss Gwilt* in April, 1876. After Henry Irving, then star member of the Lyceum Theatre company, stopped in one afternoon and saw Pinero act, he took the trouble to call on the young actor; and, when the Collins play ended its run, Irving asked him to act Claudius in *Hamlet* on tour. By December, Pinero was a member of the regular company at the Lyceum.[11]

Except for time to recover from a serious illness in 1877 and to recuperate by making a pilgrimage to every place which he had known, including Edinburgh,[12] and except for being temporarily engaged at the Globe to enact the male lead in the première of his first produced play, *Two Hundred a Year*, in October, 1877, Pinero acted at the Lyceum for the next five years. Playing in the shadow of the redoubtable Irving, he interpreted four minor roles in Shakespearean productions after his portrayal of Claudius. He acted in one eighteenth-century comedy and in eleven revivals of standard nineteenth-century plays; and he created minor roles in two new plays by established playwrights.[13] In addition, he en-

joyed the rare opportunity in the initial performances of three of
his early plays to impersonate characters which he had created.

In the fall of 1881 after another illness, he joined the Haymarket Theatre company, which was presided over by the Bancrofts.
But soon he determined to give up acting, for he had earned success with three of his own plays on the London stage. After ap-
pearing in three roles in late 1881 and early 1882, he retired,
though he came out of retirement on two later occasions. To
please the Bancrofts, he appeared as Sir Anthony Absolute in their
production of Sheridan's *The Rivals* (1884); and then to honor
them on their retirement in 1885 he acted Dolly Spanker in scenes
from Dion Boucicault's *London Assurance*.[14]

Of Pinero's qualities as an actor, two opinions were expressed
during his lifetime. One is that he was a relative failure because
he lacked fire and passion. (His Claudius was called the worst
that Birmingham had ever seen.) The other is that he was carefully attentive to details, was steady and reliable, and did well in
character parts, especially as old men and "in the silly ass type of
part." [15] Actually, both views may reflect the single fact that,
through his interest in details and in a new naturalness in acting,
he was quietly rebelling against the old declamatory style. Judged
by the old standards then prevalent in the theater, he showed no
promise of a remarkable future career as an actor. But if he could
have been judged by the standards of the newer style of acting
which his own plays came to demand, he would have been seen to
be heading, however timidly, in a new direction. When he later
coached actors in plays that he directed, he demanded naturalness
—before Stanislavski in Russia and Belasco in America. And the
fact remains that his work earned the approval of the Wyndhams,
Wilkie Collins, R. C. Carton, Henry Irving, and the Bancrofts—all
knowledgeable theater people—and that his acting was mentioned favorably by Ellen Terry.[16]

Undoubtedly, the intimate first-hand knowledge of the theater
gained from his acting experiences equipped him to be a better
playwright and director. From working in Irving's carefully regulated company he learned a businesslike approach to discipline
and rules in running a theater and in managing a company of
actors.[17] And since Irving sincerely aimed at improving theatrical
art, Pinero may also have learned from him a certain devotion to
high standards for the ensemble effect. From the roles he per-

formed he attained thorough knowledge of a variety of plays spanning three periods of English drama, and from the other side of the footlights he gained a valuable perspective on contemporary audiences' tastes.

II *His First Successes as an Author*

In 1877–78, when Pinero had made contacts inside the theatrical world, he had three scripts accepted for production. Because of his known habit of not revising scripts after completing them and because no record exists of his ever discarding a manuscript, it seems likely that these were his boyish first efforts from 1870–74 saved for the opportune moment and resurrected from the bottom of his trunk. If so, he had known in his teens how to put together a play acceptable for production—when it was presented in the right way to the right person. Rather than proving prodigious abilities on his part, however, this accomplishment may only mean that the craft was an easy one to master at the time.

The fact of production revived his desire to be a dramatist; and the interest and praise of his chief, Irving, encouraged him to write three short and four long plays while a member of the Lyceum company. In an interview in New York in 1885, Pinero acknowledged an even larger indebtedness: "I think I may fairly say that it was owing to his friendship that I persevered in playwriting. He has always been very kind to me, and I shall be grateful to him to the end of time." [18] Curiously, he never expressed his gratitude by writing a long play to exhibit Irving's talents, very likely because Irving's style was suited to grander characters than Pinero liked to draw. Moreover, Irving's management of the Lyceum is said to have done "little for the original work of contemporary English playwrights." [19]

The now ambitious young author also indulged in some nondramatic writing. In *The Theatre* of May 1, 1879, he argued for forming an organization to distribute charitable gifts to deserving impecunious actors. And in "The Inverness Cape," an autobiographical essay in *The Theatre* for August, 1880, he gave a sketch of a moody violinist who had aroused his curiosity after they met in Edinburgh in 1874. When they had become friends while working together at the Theatre Royal, the musician confessed that he had once been convicted for theft; and, on being released after serving his sentence, he had been "rescued" by a woman who offered to marry him, despite her knowledge of his crime. Through the years of his marriage, he had assumed that his wife merely pitied him; and his weighty sense of his own unworthiness led him finally to ask Pinero whether a good woman could love a "bad" man. Undoubtedly, this agonized question made the younger man ponder degrees of goodness and badness in human character; he obviously liked the man, who, though manifestly not a bad one, had been a criminal. The situation provides a parallel to many confession scenes in Pinero's plays in which a guilty person's past catches up with him in a confession, sometimes to a forgiving or compassionate friend. This narrative ends touchingly with an account of his visit to Edinburgh in 1877, when he called at the man's house to show that he still cherished the friendship. He did not have the chance, for his friend had died the day before.

Turning more and more assiduously to the composition of plays, Pinero was responding to a call for new authors issued by many writers who deplored the lack of a modern English drama and the slipshod playwriting found in English adaptations of foreign plays. In the late 1870s the protests became more outspoken, perhaps largely because the Realistic reform of T. W. Robertson and the delicate, fanciful early plays of W. S. Gilbert had given intimations of the possibilities of finer things than farces, burlesques, extravaganzas, and melodramas. In 1880, Irving complained that not many young writers seemed willing to "take the trouble to study the technique which is essential to an acting play"; [20] and Matthew Arnold urged an attempt to produce a national drama. From these opinions and criticisms, Pinero may have developed a mildly iconoclastic attitude toward the popular drama as well as an expectancy concerning the emerging drama. Not only the low status of the English drama but also the decreasing supply of foreign plays as copyright regulations became more stringent called forth the best efforts of native authors.

After 1881, as his playwriting began to take precedence over his acting, Pinero set an almost frantic pace for himself, as if making up for time lost in finding his true vocation. When he married the actress Myra Holme, a widow with a son and a daughter,[21] in 1883, he did not allow his new domestic life to slow his composition. He wrote seven full-length plays between 1882 and 1884, three of them embryonic problem plays about marriage. Dunkel describes Pinero's household arrangements during this period as trying—to the new wife.

Certainly he had little time for the social amenities in which Mrs. Pinero delighted. . . . In the morning he was a human being. And guests who were invited to see him came for luncheon and to spend the early afternoon with him. But by teatime he was restless and quite unhesitant about leaving and setting to work. . . . He began work at teatime and was not disturbed until the following morning, after he had partaken of breakfast in bed. That is, he did not have dinner with his family or take his wife out in the evening. He was working with monotonous regularity. . . . This rigid schedule he followed throughout his life.[22]

Not even Ellen Terry, who was one of the playwright's favorites, could induce him to vary this demanding routine. Echoes of the sort of discord which might be expected to arise under these circumstances appear in several plays which he wrote later, especially *Mid-Channel* (1909); and it may be no accident that he began dealing with marriage problems at this early point in his career.

At about this time he established the practice[23] of having the script of a new play printed privately and copies put into the hands of all the actors, not just the usual "sides"—portions of the text which record cues and give only the speeches of the actor concerned. This procedure served his purpose as a director interested in ensemble effect; and, when it came to be widely practiced, it helped to make Realistic acting possible.

By early 1888 Pinero had written seven more full-length pieces, among them some exceptionally popular farces for the Court Theatre and a sentimental comedy, *Sweet Lavender*. One of the farces, *The Magistrate* (1885), and *Sweet Lavender* (1888) gained him recognition abroad through translations and adaptations.[24] In connection with the original production of *The Magistrate*, he ventured into directing; and, when the London production became a success, he went to New York to rehearse Augustin Daly's company in the same play[25]—his only visit to America. For subsequent first productions of his own plays, he always occupied the director's chair and exercised rigid control over the ensemble.

III   *His Practice as Director*

Pinero's work as director significantly complemented his writing; for, as the interpreter of his plays, he could insure that their stage productions embodied his conceptions. In an interview he once stated that, if he should die after writing the full script of a new play, he would have left his work only half done. Though he thought that any dramatic author ought mentally to stage-manage every aspect of the play while composing, he insisted on going farther and conducting rehearsals himself,[26] as Robertson and Gilbert had done before him.[27]

In casting the play, Pinero was "ruthless" and "not content to take the second best or to manage with what was at once available, preferring to wait until he could obtain the best." [28] He cast according to type, perhaps the first Englishman to do so.[29] That is, he insisted that roles be distributed to actors who looked and sounded "right" for their parts. Then he passed out full scripts to all the actors and enjoined them to study the entire text, not just their own roles. In the long rehearsal period, sometimes six or seven weeks,[30] he freely prescribed intonations, facial expressions, and stage business. While he expected a seeming naturalness in the acting, he acknowledged that certain stylization was necessary; for instance, the actors had to raise their voices in order to be heard. With the artistic success of the production paramount in his mind, he did not hesitate to replace an actor who promised to be inadequate. He fully exercised his prerogatives as their master, for who knew better than he what had been the playwright's original idea and what values were to be brought out in the performances? He was demanding but courteous; and he was never so inconsiderate as George Bernard Shaw, who once kept a rehearsal in session until three o'clock in the morning.[31] In thus guiding the actors, Pinero gave them the benefit of his acting experience and of his unique knowledge of the plays. He also filled the gap created by disintegration of the old stock companies, which left young actors with no trustworthy training grounds and no particular traditions to follow.

Though actors might be expected to chafe under such trying authoritarianism, only a few attempted to have their own way; and many acknowledged Pinero's kind patience and help. After repeated proofs of his rightness, evident in the record successes of his plays and of actors and actresses in his roles, they welcomed his direction.[32] He was exceptionally fortunate in gathering into his casts performers who could give rewarding interpretations, especially Mrs. Patrick Campbell, Irene Vanbrugh, John Hare, and George Alexander.

IV Financial and Artistic Success

The farces and *Sweet Lavender* made Pinero's fame and fortune; and, after writing them, he had no choice "but to try to write great plays, regardless of the predilections of the public." [33] A play written in 1887, *The Profligate*, took him off this road of seemingly easy success onto an entirely different path. This play was his first thoroughgoing attempt to deal seriously with the problems of his time in a Realistic manner—his first true problem play. His awareness of opening wider horizons for himself and his audiences is indicated in a letter which he wrote to Clement Scott in December of that year. Gratified by the successful adaptations of *The Magistrate* in Germany, he said: ". . . I hope the time will come—is coming—when the Englishman like the Frenchman, will write his play for all nations. The consciousness, when a man is writing a play, that he is working for the amusement of a few thousand middle-class English people, is not favourable to the development of Dramatic Art." [34] This concern for a more nearly universal drama antedates any such consciousness in his nearest contemporaries in age among playwrights: Henry Arthur Jones, who only later spoke and wrote voluminously of what he called the "Renascence" of English drama, and Shaw, who had written only a portion of one play by 1887. Pinero's dedication to dramatic art suggests that his election to the Garrick Club in the same year, ten years after his debut as a playwright, was assuredly deserved.

After writing *The Profligate*, Pinero slowed his pace considerably; for he wrote only three other plays by 1891. Then he retired to the Surrey hills to study Continental masters, especially Dumas *fils*.[35] Over a period of nearly two years, he painstakingly fashioned his next work, *The Second Mrs. Tanqueray* (1893). It was this play, his twenty-eighth, which was hailed as the finest play written in England since Sheridan's *The School for Scandal* (1777) and which firmly established his reputation as a writer of serious drama; and it is the one most likely to be known by stu-

dents of the drama. For the next dozen years he could have been
challenged only by Jones for the honor of foremost playwright in
England.

After *The Second Mrs. Tanqueray* Pinero was constantly trying
to live up to its success. Before the turn of the century he wrote
five more masterful pieces: *The Notorious Mrs. Ebbsmith* (1895),
his most intellectual study of a woman who has fallen afoul of
the social code; *Trelawney of the "Wells"* (1898), his crowning
achievement in Robertsonian sentimental comedy; and three excellent comedies of manners, *The Benefit of the Doubt* (1895),
The Princess and the Butterfly (1897), and *The Gay Lord Quex*
(1899). He also undertook an insignificant collaboration with
J. Comyns Carr on the libretto for an unsuccessful romantic opera,
The Beauty Stone (1898), for which Arthur Sullivan wrote the
music. His share in it was small.[36]

After the successful production of *The Gay Lord Quex,* he
found it necessary to rest from the strain of almost incessant composition by traveling on the Continent. He left England in the
summer of 1899, spent September in the Italian lake district, win-
tered on the Riviera, and returned to England in the spring with
ideas for a new play, *Iris,* which had scenes laid in Italy. When he
had shepherded the new production onto the stage in 1901, he
took a longer rest. For a year and a half he moved around, spending "the season" of 1901 at Monte Carlo and an April in Paris; but,
by 1903, he was back in England ready to give his public another
play, *Letty,* and to make his first and only public appearance as a
literary critic when he spoke in Edinburgh on Robert Louis
Stevenson as a dramatist. In 1907 he recuperated from a serious illness by spending several months at Wiesbaden, where he occasionally lunched or dined with King Edward VII.[37]

Of the eight full-length plays which Pinero wrote between 1901
and 1912, *The Thunderbolt* (1908) and *Mid-Channel* (1909)
rank alongside *The Second Mrs. Tanqueray;* and *His House in
Order* (1906) ranks close behind. But all plays of this group have
an almost classic simplicity; with great verisimilitude, their settings and actions picture a number of different locales and types
in Edwardian society. They reflect Pinero's acquaintance with the
world outside the theater, a world in which he was now comfortable and respected. In 1909, he became the second man of letters

(Gilbert was the first) to be knighted for his services to dramatic literature.

But, by 1910, there was a new generation of playgoers who were unaware of Pinero's triumphs in the 1880s and 1890s; Shaw had attracted a loyal public, J. M. Barrie's works had become popular, and such younger playwrights as John Galsworthy and Somerset Maugham were emerging. The kind of plays which Pinero could write best were no longer avant-garde; and, by 1912, when he produced The *"Mind the Paint" Girl*, audiences irreverently booed and hissed in the middle of scenes.[38]

Furthermore, changes associated with the passing of the Edwardian era and the outbreak of World War I help to explain why his works suffered a decline in popularity. The theater remained prosperous during the years 1914–18; but light entertainment, not Shakespeare or gentlemanly Realism, made it so.[39] Pinero even changed the ending of one of his plays, *The Big Drum* (1915), to cater to the new mood of wartime audiences. The actor-managers of an earlier era disappeared and made way for theatrical speculators; and Pinero could no longer count upon automatically placing a play with an old friend, since John Hare had retired in 1911 and George Alexander produced few plays between 1911 and his death in 1918. By the end of the war, the theater, formerly a popular one, had become a domain of smaller, more sophisticated audiences; the crowds had shifted their patronage to the movies.[40]

For a time, Pinero had nothing impressive to offer London audiences. He seemed to have written himself out. Additionally, the war evidently crushed his spirits and hampered inspiration. His ordinarily stoic nature and great energies suffered another setback when Lady Pinero, who had for years regulated his household so that he could devote himself almost entirely to the theater, died after a long illness in 1919. He felt the loss so strongly that composition seemed almost impossible.[41] In the fifteen years by which he outlived her he wrote only five long and two short plays; yet the long plays evince no lack of inventiveness and no decline in technical skill.

Surprisingly, when Pinero was in his sixties, he found the courage to attempt experiments. Having employed a mildly Expressionistic technique to stage the appearance and disappearance of a ghost in a one-act play in 1912, he abandoned straightforward

verisimilitude in several fantasies. In *Mr. Livermore's Dream*
(1917) and in *The Enchanted Cottage* (1922) he used pageant-
like sequences representing dreams. In *The Freaks* (1918) he employed obvious distortion; and in *Dr. Harmer's Holidays* (written
1923–24), he adopted episodic construction and included, as his
final scene, a tableau resembling a "still" from a silent movie. However, his flexibility in these plays has never been analyzed by commentators.

V *"Theatricality" in His Writing*

During Pinero's long and varied career spanning more than
sixty years, a theatrical atmosphere was the air he breathed—even
in lawyers' offices, in an Edinburgh boardinghouse, on a Surrey
farmstead, or in travels in Italy. It was in the theater that he met
his actress-wife; they shared a theatrical career for a time after
their marriage until he insisted that she retire from the stage. His
friends belonged to the theater world: to the Bancrofts he was
always loyal, and Ellen Terry frequently visited in his home.
Edmund Gosse and William Archer, both interested in English
drama as critics and as champions of Ibsen, were "as close to Pinero
as anyone could be." [42] His acquaintances included Gilbert and
Sullivan, Henry Arthur Jones, Barrie, and Shaw. In addition he
knew T. W. Robertson the younger, and he worked with Dion
Boucicault the younger. His relations with actor-manager George
Alexander grew to a warm friendship, and he was on cordial
terms with the entrepreneur Charles Frohman. Among his recorded friendships stand few names of persons not connected
with the theater, though Hamilton Fyfe insists that Pinero's clos-
est friends were men of varied interests and occupations. One of
these was Marshall Hall, a noted criminal lawyer;[43] and another
was Sir Thomas Sutherland, a ship owner, who frequently invited
the playwright to join him on the trial runs of new ships.[44]

Pinero's devotion to the theater is exemplified in his withdrawal
from social activities to follow an austere method of composition.
The starting point of a play, for him, was a vision of certain characters who invited him to investigate them. Having received such
an invitation, he usually retired for three or four months, frequently to the country, to become acquainted with these creatures
of his imagination. He spoke of them as if they were real people:

"When they talk, I listen to them; when they act, I watch them; when they wait, I have to wait for them. Of course, if they bestir themselves at dinner time, I have no dinner." [45] Having decided what they would do when brought together, he constructed a scenario for the entire play, took a short vacation, and then wrote the dialogue. On finishing each act, he sent it to the printers; for it required no additional revision. Then he rushed forward to direct the rehearsals.[46]

When Pinero "vacationed," he went to one of his clubs or to a cricket match; or, less often, he traveled. Never a publicity seeker, he scorned in two plays, *The Big Drum* (1915) and *Child Man* (published 1930), those who contrived to be much in the public eye. His view of the artist's role emerges from the circumstance that writers in his plays are never seen at their work; they write in the next room or upstairs while life goes on without them. Even after he had the means to be comfortable and gregarious, he remained somewhat withdrawn, composing plays and directing them. As St. John Ervine has said, ". . . he bore his prosperity with as much fortitude as his adversity." [47]

Pinero's love of the theater would not have been stronger had he come from a theatrical family. Looking back on his beginnings in its "magical" realm, he identified those days with salvation from the boredom of legal routine and from his middle-class background. Yet since he had come to the theater as an outsider, he was all the more ready to break away from its stereotypes and clichés. When he first began to be critical, he criticized or parodied outworn theatrical conventions; later, he attacked social conventions. Among the outcast artists of the Victorian theater, he first tasted ostracism and thereby found a subject which he found viable in plays dealing with the large world—loss of reputation. In two mature plays, *Trelawney of the "Wells"* and *The "Mind the Paint" Girl*, both written well after the social status of the acting profession had improved, he depicted the mingling of the theater's artists with the upper classes; and in both, the world of the theater expands to be more nearly commensurate with the surrounding one, reflecting Pinero's experience of escaping the narrowness of a purely theatrical way of looking at life. Voicing what he had long before realized, one of his heroines, the actress Rose Trelawney, observes, "It isn't *the* world we [actors] live in, merely *a* world—such a queer little one!" The imputation of a restrictive theatricality in Pinero's writing is applicable only to certain early plays, for the bigger world outside the theater finally became his larger stage.

CHAPTER 2

Fledgling Playwright

THE ten plays which Pinero wrote before 1882, the year of his retirement from acting, are tentative efforts in which the emerging playwright had not exactly found his métier. But in writing them he assimilated what his reading, his theatergoing, and his acting experiences could teach him; and by experimenting he also marked out the course of his future development and in some measure the course of late nineteenth-century English drama.

As an actor he had appeared in revivals of Shakespeare and in the old-fashioned poetic tragedies of James Sheridan Knowles and Edward Bulwer-Lytton, but he was also aware that hardly any plays being written in his time followed the tragic scheme. Hence it is not surprising that he did not attempt tragedy early in his career. He had acted in melodramas of the older type popular since 1800 and in Irving's melodramatic starring vehicle, *The Bells*. Considering the vogue for melodrama, which only slightly declined in the 1870s, he might have been wise to found a career by capitalizing on it; but, somewhat surprisingly, he studiously avoided melodramatic plotting except in an isolated scene or two and altogether eschewed melodramatic character drawing. He had taken a role in at least one standard farcical afterpiece and had opportunity to see numerous farcical plays written by W. G. Wills and H. J. Byron; but when he wrote farcically he attempted to go beyond their obvious tricks and puns. On the whole, Pinero showed a distinct preference for comedy, which in the 1870s had acquired a new light dialogue along with a "modern" tone and some psychological study of motivation, but which in general retained a rosy coloring of sentiment. In this genre Robertson was Pinero's model. In whatever genre he was writing at this time, however, Pinero did not rely heavily on the method of the French "well-made" play, a method involving compression of the time-

25

scheme so that a great deal of the story is merely told about, often in rapid exposition; emphasis on well-oiled plot machinery at the expense of character probing; structuring acts and scenes to rise to exciting climaxes; and a seemingly logical sequence of events. He could have absorbed the technique when he appeared in Victorien Sardou's *Odette* or when he acted in James Albery's *Jingle,* a "well-made" adaptation of Dickens's *The Pickwick Papers;* but few English authors had set an example of employing it.[1]

Since only three of Pinero's ten preliminary efforts were ever published—and those not until well after 1891, when the United States gave copyright protection to works by foreign authors—critics, lacking texts, have dismissed them as insignificant. The fact that most of them were not published does not in itself imply their worthlessness, however; for publication under copyright laws which did not yet safeguard against piracy in American theaters would have been foolish. The plays exist among the Lord Chamberlain's manuscripts deposited for licensing, now housed in the British Museum. Their style reveals Pinero's use of dramatic conventions, and their variety shows his eagerness to experiment. They afford evidence to support or disprove certain critical assumptions about his outlook and originality in later plays (for example, the assumption of his indebtedness to Ibsen), and they provide a bench mark for measuring the artistic peaks which he later reached.

I *Two Curtain Raisers*

Pinero's first play to reach the stage was a comedietta (a short, lightly comic rather than farcical play) called *Two Hundred per Annum* in the manuscript and alternately *Two Hundred a Year* or *Two Hundred Pounds a Year.* In its only recorded performance, as a curtain raiser at London's Globe Theatre on October 6, 1877,[2] Pinero took one of the four roles, that of Jack Meadows, who has a gentlemanly interest in clothes, good food, and cigars, as well as good humor and a stoical willingness to adjust to adverse circumstances. This somewhat heroic stoicism works a change in the heroine, who is of chief interest in this slight piece. Flora, Jack's bride of two weeks, is an unconventional, independent girl who has married him in the hope of being saved from the annoyance of fortune-seeking suitors and in the expectation of dominating him by simply giving him money to indulge his tastes. Her anomalous position as the domineering "new woman" suddenly collapses when she learns that the cash and securities which she expected to inherit immediately cannot be located. Faced with the prospect of living on Jack's meager income, she laments her lost luxury and authority; but, when she sees how stoically he faces the loss, she no longer thinks of him as "a weak, mean-spirited poor man." Moved to emulate his attitude, she abruptly becomes hopeful of a new life, even of the romantic love which she has told him not to expect. By the time obvious authorial maneuvers bring about a superfluous happy reversal of circumstances, giving her the fortune after all, she is sure that she wants only her Jack and his "two hundred a year."

The plot deals with such ordinary concerns as marital adjustment and maintenance of comfort and status and with lawyers and wills. Yet, unlike farce, this comic play evinces Pinero's strong interest in the effect of one character upon another. There is some telling psychological insight in Jack's stooping—just once—to tell Flora all that he could reproach her with if he were not a gentleman. The dialogue is suited to the characters, especially Jack's language, which is more rhetorical than Flora's because of his being a student of the law. On the whole, the play is quite successful according to the conventions of the era; but it also has a spark of originality in the character of Flora.

The other play which represented the novice on the London stage in the 1877–78 season was another one-act piece, *Two Can Play at That Game*. Its performance at the Lyceum in May with Pinero in the cast brought him five pounds as royalty and later elicited encouragement from Irving.[3] It details some crucial moments in the honeymoon of Montgomery and Kate Clutterbuck. Montgomery, acting on the advice of a nautical friend, the redoubtable Captain Joe Bunyard, who has had an unhappy experience of married life, decides to test Kate's love for him: he will tell her that he is much older and more infirm than she suspects, hinting that he married her to gain free nursing. But Kate, who has overheard their plans, adroitly turns the tables by pretending to have deceived him: she says that she has been married before, to a Captain Joe Bunyard; and she does not know whether she is now wife, widow, or bigamist. Before Montgomery collapses, a confrontation of the three principals clears away misunderstandings; and the play ends foolishly with the title echoed almost operatically in crude doggerel.

With its emphasis on reversal of situation, the piece has the plot of a farce; but it is considerably above mere clowning in its light treatment of marital adjustment and in its pleasant use of comic irony: each mate elaborates his false confession with relish, and Kate's possessing superior knowledge characterizes her as more attractive than the cringing men.

II   *First Full-length Play*

Perhaps because the third play, Pinero's first full-length effort, was never produced in London, it has been omitted from certain bibliographies. Entitled first *Paul Marston's Love* and then *La Comète; or, Two Hearts,* it had one obscure production at the Theatre Royal in Croydon, just south of London, in April, 1878.[4] Its quality suggests that it may have been the play earlier rejected as being "of no earthly use." In its prologue and three tiresome acts, it recalls some details of both *Camille* and *A Tale of Two Cities* as it recounts the romantic story of young Paul Marston, scion of an old English family, and his love for a *déclassée* Parisian *danseuse,* La Comète, a married woman who mistakenly thinks her husband is dead. After a well-meaning family friend has separated the lovers in the Prologue, the first act poses a nice dilemma: shall old Sir John Marston allow his son to die of a gunshot wound received in a hunting accident, complicated by grief for his lost love, or shall he accede to the doctor's wish that the "tainted" woman be summoned to give Paul the desire to recover? Though Sir John refuses to send for her, on moral grounds rather than from class snobbery, she coincidentally appears at the Marston estate. Promising help, she asks the doctor to keep Paul alive for a week and leaves. In a crudely repetitious and roundabout second act, she dons a nun's habit and resorts to the incredibly simple expedient of fetching her long-lost twin sister from a French village without revealing her own identity or her reasons. And in the third act, the cure succeeds: Paul falls in love with the "pure" twin and begins to recover; and La Comète, sounding like Sydney Carton in her curtain line, renounces the world with "all its beauty, joy, and sin" and departs for a convent.

This juvenile fantasy of a sacrificial love that restores health and clears away all obstacles to union with at least the image of the fallen woman expresses attitudes which underlie much less optimistic later plays by Pinero. Sir John's rigidity remains an inescapable fact, but Paul is fortunately not bent to his father's will, nor is the fascinating Magdalen punished; therefore, propriety is satisfied at the same time that happiness is guaranteed. This most far-fetched of all Pinero's solutions sidesteps all the issues, in its youthful ignorance. In using disguise, in introducing low-comic rascals, and in drawing his major characters, the young writer was largely derivative; but in his attempt at creating the local color of a Paris tavern and in his detailed and architecturally valid settings, he was more nearly original.

III Daisy's Escape

The praise which Irving had for *Two Can Play at That Game* inspired Pinero to write his next play, the comedietta *Daisy's Escape*, presented September 20, 1879. After the performance Irving gave him a handsome royalty of fifty pounds and prophesied a bright future for him if he kept on in the same way.[5]

The basis of the action in *Daisy's Escape* is the comic failure of an eloping couple to adjust to each other under the trying conditions created by a snowstorm. The young woman, Daisy White, has impulsively run away from her stuffy old guardian because she wants a new life; but, while their train is snowbound, she realizes that life with her prospective husband, Augustus Caddel, would be even worse. By a purely expedient choice of a more desirable man, a former beau who by chance reenters her life, she escapes a horrible future. The plot also guarantees some good laughs at the expense of Caddel, the comic villain.

Daisy, though less spirited and less romantic than the earlier heroines, is a fuller portrait of the emerging Pineroesque woman. Throughout the play, she is governed by impulse and motivated by self-interest and her desire for comfort and happiness. When she must take the "damp point of view" of the world, she almost breaks down. In one aside, she paradoxically advises girls always to elope in the summertime to avoid the cold and wet. The role, according to Dunkel, who had interviews with Pinero, was played by Myra Holme, later Mrs. Pinero, though a review of the first performance lists another actress in the role.[6]

Augustus Caddel, whose name suggests his chief trait and

whose eccentricities afforded Pinero—in a red wig—an acting
success, is a vulgar, rude, self-centered, ill-tempered son of a
wealthy brewer; but he has only seventy pounds a year of his
own. He chides Daisy for sulkiness, asks her to help him remove
his coat, and cautions her to "mind the fur." Offended by her lack
of gratitude for what he has done for her, he reminds her that he
has "been at considerable expense and trouble over the affair." He
neglects to order her any refreshments and then smokes a pipe in
her presence without asking her permission. A new type for
Pinero, Caddel became the basis for some of his later bourgeois
characters. In contrast, Tom Rossiter, who wins Daisy, is wealthy,
gentle, and generous.

The diction of the play moves toward metaphorical consistency
in that frustration is repeatedly expressed in terms of discomfort:
cheap shoes that cannot be stretched; dampness; cold. Pinero here
made his first symbolic use of properties. When the shivering
Daisy is offered Augustus's fur coat to warm her, she replies, "No,
dear. [N]ot that, the fur is so irritating [.] Fetch me the light
wrap [Tom's] over there [.] It's nicer."

IV Bygones

By December, 1879, Pinero had finished *Bygones,* a one-act
comedy with a rural setting and a new infusion of sentiment. But
the play did not mount the stage until Irving produced it in September, 1880, when the author acted the most interesting role,
that of Professor Mazzoni, the singing-master.[7] The plot concerns
an innocent country girl, Ruby, who is loved by Curzon Gram-
shawe, son of the most honored family in the county; but out of
disillusionment and pride, he rejects her when he discovers that
she is not truly the daughter of the rector. Out of pique, she then
agrees to marry her much older singing-master, an exiled Italian
nobleman, who has loved her while watching her grow up and
who appreciates her true worth. When her young beau reverses
his decision and returns to claim her, she seems for a moment to
be in a quandary; but, in another reversal, the singing-master,
having realized his folly in hoping for rejuvenation through love,
removes the complication by nobly giving her up. His going away
to Italy tinges the otherwise happy resolution with Robertsonian
pathos.

Again, Pinero's plot centers on the woman's proper or improper choice between two suitors, but it is considerably strengthened by the two themes which guide its development: ability to adjust to disillusionment and the contrast between genuine and spurious nobility.

Fuller characterization is given some of the characters than is called for by the plot. Giles Horncastle, the first Pineroesque churchman (leaving the French curate in *La Comète* out of account), has a certain unstereotyped unorthodoxy that survives in later clerics. Otherwise a worthy man, he has been deceitful about Ruby's parentage. He also has the subsidiary trait of interest in archeology and ecclesiastical architecture. Professor Mazzoni, though he has rather artificial dialogue, is given fullest characterization—a music teacher, philosopher, inventor, he is also a man of principle and of noble impulse. He has knowledge of law, and he helps Horncastle to word his will. As Pinero's first older man who rivals a younger one for a woman's love, he makes a heroic renunciation.

The play attempts to use consistent imagery, and it employs offstage music not as a device to whip up excitement but as ironic counterpoint to the onstage action: Ruby's happy singing offstage, as the professor is leaving, heightens the bittersweetness of the ending.

V Girls and Boys

Soon after meeting Myra Holme in 1879, Pinero began a full-length play[8] in which she created the leading role in its belated production. Originally called *Human Nature: A Village Love Story*, it was produced as *Girls and Boys: A Nursery Tale* (1882). Perhaps he wrote it to display her particular talents or was inspired by her to create the heroine; at any rate, it was his boldest experiment to date. Keeping the rural setting of *Bygones,* he mingled ordinary farce, genial Dickensian sentiment, and a serious presentation of his own kind of sympathetic but tarnished heroine, though the mixture was inartistic. Undoubtedly, Pinero, taking a more critical look at the conventions, decided that hard and fast distinctions between genres could not be maintained once the playwright committed himself to dealing with contemporary life faithfully. Certain critics of the day deplored the crea-

tion of bastard genres by the mixture of tones; but more recent
readers, accustomed to dark comedy as written by Chekhov and
others, do not object.

Unaccustomed to the requirements of the longer play, Pinero
complicated the plot with a major story line and two lesser ones;
and he repeatedly followed this three-stranded formula in later
compositions. (More common among plays of the period was a
single strand of intrigue or a double plot featuring two sets of
characters, high and low.) The major plot features Gillian West, a
worldly, dissatisfied woman who gives up a somewhat disreputable occupation as a horse trainer and a circus rider to find contentment as a respectable villager. When an obviously desirable
young man, Mark Avory, falls in love with her, she realizes that
Mark's guardian would disinherit him for forming such a misalliance; and she renounces her chance of happiness. She accepts instead the proposal of the wise, genial, but in many ways ridiculous
cobbler-schoolmaster Solomon Protheroe. But, before the wedding can take place, Mark returns from a Grand Tour, impoverished and ill. Since now a misalliance cannot ruin Mark, Gillian
impulsively rejects security with Solomon to marry Mark. The fact
that she will take him despite his poverty mollifies his guardian,
who consents to the match and gives her a dowry.

The characters in the subplots act mindlessly in their readiness
to marry, seemingly to bring about a happy ending. They have no
place in a play which pretends to have artistic fidelity to life and
to portray realistically a credible woman character who faces a
real dilemma. Beside Gillian, they are absurd; and the two modes,
one conventional, one original, clash mightily.

The diction of two characters is worthy of comment. Solomon's
pretentious language seems to give some support to the uncritical
generalization that Pinero wrote with a too literary flavor. Solomon talks of the human heart as "the undiscovered continent,"
"the north pole of humanity." He tells Mark that if he must marry,
he ought to find a "tip top patent leather single soled, hand
stitched lady and not a machine made nondescript." On the other
hand, Gillian's plain, worldly talk seems to support the contention
that Pinero was a vulgarian and lacked an ear for "civilized" conversation. When she is warned that Mark is not one of her privi-
leges as Solomon's tenant, she replies, "Put him down in the bill
then. I'm going in for luxuries." In replying to Solomon's marriage

proposal, she says, "I've seen too much of hard times in my life to consider [the question in regard to true love], and it's better to wrangle with a man over a hot joint than to love him on a thin slice of bread-and-butter." The language of each is exactly in character, and the language of neither should be assumed to exhaust the author's capabilities.

VI Hester's Mystery

Pinero wrote one more short play before turning exclusively to long ones. In May, 1880, he finished *Hester's Mystery*, a comedietta which was performed soon after.[9] Like *Bygones* and *Girls and Boys*, it has a rural setting; in this case, the farm of the widow Butterworth, where her daughter Hester is expected home from school. Mystery intrudes when the headmaster appears and reveals in an aside that Hester had left school six weeks earlier. When Hester appears, he threatens to disgrace her unless she gives him a friendly kiss; but she cleverly retorts that he must be trying to trick her into forfeiting her good-conduct award. When he hints that she may already not deserve it, she confesses her secret marriage to John Royle, only recently hired as a farmhand, who appears and corroborates her story. Mrs. Butterworth, who out of bitterness has always cautioned Hester to stay away from men, threatens to send her away as a disgraced woman; but Hester produces a baby which she and John proclaim to be theirs. In a contrived and sentimental ending, the sight of the baby mollifies the widow; and she vows much too suddenly to be a kind grandmother. The schoolmaster departs meekly, and the play ends with the customary tableau of those remaining. Here, ironically, the daughter's disobedience, which results from following natural instincts, changes the mother to a woman who is no longer tart-tongued, shrewish, and embittered. Society's code remains intact (Hester has been married for nearly a year), the mother's too strict version of it is modified, and the girl gains happiness.

The women alone in this play show unconventional characterization, for the males are stock figures. Nance Butterworth, through imaginative and interesting diction, becomes so much the shrew that her sudden change at the end is not credible. Hester, the pretty, spirited candidate for a good-conduct medal, clearly violates expected propriety by being revealed as a deceitful and undutiful daughter. But, absolved by confession and by her mother's forgiveness, she loses her supposed taint. In later plays, Pinero's heroines never even hope to win good-conduct awards.

The stage directions indicate Pinero's most thorough concern to date for stage managing the whole performance; in them he evinces unwillingness to leave the effects to the usual stereotyped casting and to the usual stock scenery. He gives promise of becoming the thoroughgoing Realist and autocratic director of later years. He lavishes attention on the insignificant Joel by describing him as an "old farm laborer, with straggling grey hair and a withered face" who "wears a dirty smock-frock, worsted stockings, and very large heavy boots." And he specifies minutely the practical and merely atmospheric details of the scene: a scrub-brush to be thrown at Joel, an iron pail and a pump handle used by the actors, and real straw, butter tubs, and milk cans for verisimilitude. The whole scene was "to be quaint and old-fashioned, and as bright as possible." The demand for brightness foreshadows his concern later for realistic lighting; but, after the adoption of electricity in 1881, he never needed to call for mere brightness again.

VII   The Money-Spinner

A two-act play, *The Money-Spinner* (1880), became Pinero's first hit. Its successful tryout in November at Manchester's Theatre Royal guaranteed its moving on, in early 1881, to London's St. James's Theatre,[10] where he achieved several later triumphs. In the plot of this comedy which is centered on money and love, the sympathetically presented heroine, Millie Boycott, is given a chance to save her embezzler husband Harold from exposure by a detective. Not shocked when he confesses the truth to her, she prepares to help him by employing tricks to cheat at cards that she had learned in her father's gambling casino; and, thereby, she becomes again the money-spinner. In her attempt to swindle a guest who was formerly her suitor but is now her sister's she is discovered by the detective. The guest, Lord Kengussie, because he still loves her, connives at her trickery and saves her honor by nobly giving money to make up the husband's deficit. Carefully avoiding a melodramatic unmasking of Millie and any outburst of emotion, the ending keeps resolutely to the comic mode with a comic thwarting of the detective.

A recitation of the story line such as this hardly does justice to the play or indicates how it was unusual in its time. It was the freshness of characterization that marked Pinero as promising. Harold Boycott, for instance, is no ordinary hero; basically upright, and concerned with lifting his wife to his respectable level, he has nevertheless committed a crime, though in mitigating circumstances. He speaks to his father-in-law, "Baron" Croodle, with un-Victorian candor and lack of respect (deserved, admittedly). Millie, his wife, is a Pineroesque woman portrayed at a later stage than usual: already married, she has left her unpleasant past behind. Her character deepens when she must decide whether or not to act dishonorably in her new life, thus recalling a past which she would rather forget. In an apology which comes near expressing a deterministic philosophy, she speaks of her early environment as having made her a cheat, so that it is easier for her to sin than to take the right course.

Lord Kengussie at first seems a conventional character whose sentiment and forgetfulness are his major traits; but his forgetting only Millie's husband's name suggests that his lingering affection for her has created a real mental block and gives him somewhat more psychological depth. Dorinda, Millie's sister, shows how coarse and slangy Millie might have been. Kengussie has insisted on a year's "finishing" for her before their wedding. Their father, the spurious baron, is another idler, a coarse buffoon rather more conventionally drawn. The detective, relatively new in literature at the time, cannot really be called a stereotyped character, especially since Pinero drew him as a near villain not only bent on disclosure of the hero's misdeed but also determined to ruin a woman's honor by meddling.

To Pinero's contemporaries, the play seemed to have a "notable acting quality" and the characterization was "deft and vigorous." In this respect alone, it "attracted a whole generation" of imitators.[11]

VIII Imprudence

Pinero's second success on the London stage in 1881, *Imprudence,* continued in the same vein of characterization; and it earned reproach from at least one critic for the low estimate of human nature which it reflected.[12] The action of this farce-comedy of boardinghouse manners pictures life in "Lazenby's High Class Boarding Establishment," and it deals boisterously with the concerns of its middle-class London occupants. Pinero was probably painting from life, recalling his acquaintances in an Edinburgh theatrical boardinghouse; but he fortunately did not use his setting merely to bring together a collection of zany types.

But in plotting, *Imprudence* was experimental, making considerable advance over the earlier experiments in *Girls and Boys*. Varying somewhat the formula for a three-stranded plot, he did not allow any one strand of the story to take prominence; instead of having a major plot, he let all the incidents develop a major theme, that imprudent behavior stems from frustration. In being theme-centered rather than plot-centered, *Imprudence* suggests the practice of Chekhov, though, unlike Chekhov, Pinero is not concerned in this play with the delicate inner essences of his characters.

Though no character can be said to be central in importance, there is a "device" character, Durant, who unites the three threads of the plot, all revealed in the first act: (1) Mr. Dalrymple, retired from public service in India, commissions Durant to find a man who will take his spinsterish daughter Zaida off his hands so that he can pose as a younger man and remarry. (2) George Castleton, thinking that his fiancée has just spurned him, gives Durant a similar commission because he must immediately find a wife or lose an inheritance. Naturally, Durant begins to encourage a match between Castleton and Zaida Dalrymple; but this simple solution is thwarted by the buffoonish stratagems of Parminter Blake. (3) Though the Blakes, married less than a year, have come to London for a more active social life, Parminter is now disenchanted with the flirtatious Marie's great success in attracting the attention of the other male boarders. In order to quench their ardor, he circulates the rumor that his marriage was never legalized, thinking that the men will withdraw on hearing of her disgrace. But Castleton, urgently needing a wife, proposes to her without consulting Durant. Authorial maneuvers to bring characters together in the dining room at midnight and to keep various ones out of each other's way dominate and flaw the second act.

In the third act, Blake, forced by the scandals of the night to confess his hoax, forgives Marie's "flow of animal spirits"; and she repents her flirtatiousness. In this truly comic ending to their story, both are chastened and no longer ridiculous; and they vow to return to the country. More farcically, Castleton's situation changes—he finds that his fiancée still loves him; and, assured of

his inheritance, he offers to treat his fellow boarders and the landlady to a good meal, for a change. There is also a conventional
pairing off of Durant and Zaida. Durant, seeing Zaida's determination to earn her bread and bonnets, proposes marriage as an
alternative. Having impulsively, perhaps imprudently, accepted
him, she turns unexpectedly to her detested father and trium-
phantly disowns him in another instance of the tables turned.
Love, youth, and sanity succeed in this happy ending with a
comic vengeance.

With frustrations removed, all appropriately anticipate the catered dinner; for frustration and bad cuisine have been metaphor-
ically linked since the opening lines, where the landlady protests
that life is "one perpetual cold joint—a vale of breakages . . . of
brass buttons and iron nails found in the soup." Much of the action precedes or follows a meal, suggesting the ordinary routine in
a boardinghouse. The script requires no musical effects and is thus
less theatrical, mirroring perhaps more faithfully the actual, dull
reality.

IX   The Squire

In December, Pinero had his third success of 1881 with *The
Squire*.[13] Following its opening at the St. James's, a controversy
arose concerning the possibility that he had plagiarized its characters and setting and certain of its situations from Thomas Hardy's
Far From the Madding Crowd. The playwright finally felt moved
to defend himself by contributing to a symposium in *The Theatre*
for February, 1882. Denying that he had read Hardy's novel before the play was written, he pointed out that as much as two
years before *The Squire* he had already turned to the lanes and
hedgerows for settings similar to Hardy's, as *Hester's Mystery* and
Girls and Boys show. And, by publishing a memorandum from his
notebook, he proved the genesis of the play in his own mind, not
Hardy's. Truly, the actual similarity between the two works is
slight. The memorandum shows that Pinero had started with a
melodramatic situation involving a heroine who *seems* guilty and
also with a difficult craftsman's problem in regard to the denouement: "The notion of a young couple secretly married—the girl
about to become a mother—finding that a former wife is still in
existence. The heroine amongst those who respect and love her.
The fury of a rejected lover who believes her to be a guilty

woman. Two men face to face at night-time. Q[uer]y—Kill the
first wife?" [14] Clearly, he had at first considered an unorthodox
conclusion, but later he must have found that he could not manage it.

The play begins well. Like Pinero's earlier plays it gives prominence to the "guilty" woman, Kate Verity, but at a later stage,
after she has already made her choice of mates. Her entrance,
skillfully prepared for, gives a pleasant shock in revealing that she
is the Squire. The exposition, which occupies most of the first two
acts, reveals her respected position in the community; her rejection of the strapping foreman, Gilbert Hythe, who admires and
loves her; her secret marriage to Lt. Eric Thorndyke; and her
pregnancy. In Act Two, Eric decides to reveal their marriage to
save her reputation, though by doing so he will lose his mother's
fortune (she has stipulated that he must not marry during her
lifetime). In a climactic scene the two are found together at night
by Gilbert Hythe, who threatens to kill Eric. Melodramatically,
Kate saves Eric by identifying him as her husband and as the
father of her unborn child, and the act ends with a conventional
tableau.

The third act, also disappointing, brings added complication. A
mysterious and sickly foreign lady whose arrival at the local inn
has been commented on in the first act has revealed herself to the
"mad" local parson as Eric's deserted first wife. Parson Dormer,
already a woman hater, threatens to publish Kate's shame at a
harvest festival; but, conveniently, the foreigner's death saves the
day. Through this turn of events Kate, who has been ready to go
away to prevent disgrace, can now join Eric as his legal wife when
he departs for India. Regrettably, Pinero took the easy way to
solve the problem he began with; and the ending does not fulfill
the promise of the memorandum or the natural air of the first act.
But the ending is not completely syrupy: Eric and Kate will be
relatively poor because of the lost inheritance. There is only a hint
of a subplot, a story parallel to Kate's in which one of the servants
falls in love with a sergeant in Eric's regiment but is deserted by
him.

The characterization is less forward-looking than the plotting.
Eric is basically the stock well-intentioned lover; he has assumed
his first wife to be dead. His predicament arises because he is a
victim of his own past. Kate exhibits likeness to other Victorian

heroines in her chagrin at not being able to discourage Gilbert Hythe's proposals and in her concern over her would-be disgrace. Hythe, because of his robustness, reliability, and reticence, does indeed seem Hardyesque. Parson Dormer, the most original character, has traits that are unnecessary in relation to the plot: he is uncouth and slovenly, calls himself a "truth-teller," and hints at a very unhappy love in his past, which perhaps accounts for his lack of charity toward his leading parishioner, Kate. There is also an extraneous, disagreeable newspaper reporter who tipples. The picture is filled in with stock rustics and a stagy gypsy waiting-woman to Kate, along with her no-good dipsomaniacal brother.

Especially noteworthy is the prominence of local color in the various farcical appearances of the rude countrymen, in the harvest festivities, and in the stage settings. The stage set for the first act is unusually solid architecturally for its time, representing an old archway in the courtyard of Kate's manor house, above which is Kate's room. Later there is an almost cinematic shift of points of view: having created a mystery surrounding that room over the arch in the first act, the playwright takes his audience inside it for succeeding acts. Also, music is used well, especially in the second act, when a song about faithless soldier-lovers ironically punctuates the action, and in the third act, when the harvesters sing an authentic folk song.

The tone of the play embraces farce, in the "low" characters; melodrama, in the climax of the second act; and the truly serious, in Kate's third-act situation. The ending is a contrived, sentimentally happy one; and the entire piece was labeled "comedy" by the author. Though on the whole an artistic failure, the play has often been referred to as its author's first attempt at *drame moderne;* it gives some promise of his later quality. Fyfe could praise *The Squire* as the first piece in which Pinero steadily mirrored nature,[15] but Allardyce Nicoll was willing only to give Pinero credit for sincerely trying in it to advance the drama beyond Robertson's achievement and for relating the characters of his imagination to the social life of his day.[16]

X *Significance of the Early Plays*

These early pieces made successful use of traditional methods and had sufficient novelty to catch the attention of both audiences and critics. They are important for having given Pinero a chance to be noticed and for illustrating the early development of his peculiar talents for plotting and characterization. Judged by standards of the time, they are quite acceptable pieces; judged by the later standards which Pinero himself set, most of them are tame, awkward, and unrealistic.

In the five longer plays of this group Pinero gave plot greater depth and variety than was usual in farce or melodrama, as if he were striving after the fullness of the novel. He wrote neither pure farce nor pure melodrama, but he showed "deftness" [17] in both serious situations and light comedy. However, in *Girls and Boys* and in *The Squire* he failed to blend comic and serious material in a satisfying way. In the climactic scenes of *The Money-Spinner* and *The Squire*, he went beyond the tame Robertsonian style in creating strong effects but at the same time did not slavishly imitate the French "well-made" play. His experimentation with a "three-track" scheme for plotting produced one multilayered, theme-centered play, *Imprudence*, and further demonstrated his freedom from the French influence.

In characterization, he showed even more originality. From the first, he was interested in giving adequate motivation and in showing the effect of one character upon another. There were few people writing in the 1870s who could have taught him this feat since only a few had begun "to evoke dramatic excitement out of ordinary thoughts and commonplace motives." [18] Except in the farces, the major characters act as if they were surrounded by real wills or minds, not merely stage stereotypes. In all but the farcical plots and subplots, he characteristically showed characters changing, though the changes are sometimes crudely managed. His character portrayals attracted notice for their hint of freshness. Without reading Emile Zola—before Zola's collected essays on Naturalism in the drama appeared, in fact—Pinero developed a healthy horror of "the merely sympathetic personage." Archer attributed to him the aim of giving his creations real character, both good and bad qualities; and he also defended Pinero against the charge of cynicism by suggesting that the real cynic is one who says that characters with any tinge of goodness are repellent. [19] Realizing that stage stereotypes were not the genuine representatives of the human species that he had met in lawyers' offices and in the theater, Pinero tried from the start to break down those stereotypes. His characters were not new to literature, but they

were new to the stage of his day. In later plays, the increasingly
more convincing characterization led to less obvious contrivance
in plotting.

That Pinero's every hero and every heroine have these mixed
qualities suggests that he had come to a settled view of human
nature, an unidealized one, by 1882 when he was twenty-seven.
He did not shrink from the weaknesses and errors that he knew
people possessed, and he presented them with a Realist's detachment. He seemed fascinated by the putative or actual loss of reputation of certain women, the hint of scandal in the past, or the
falsity of an undeserved social position. In his later plays, this interest recurs so frequently that one critic has suggested that
Pinero created with it a whole new genre—the "drama of reputation." [20] He touched once or twice on marital discord, but he comically resolved the difficulties. Cherishing no Romantic notions
about the natural goodness of women, Pinero drew them as willful and unconventional. His women do not mindlessly follow a
code of behavior but are more sentient and more impulsive creatures than the men. On occasion, however, they are capable of a
heroic gesture or true sacrifice. They seldom appear with mother,
guardian, or chaperone; and, in their financial independence, they
recall the fact that women were just winning the right to hold
property in Victorian England.

By drawing his male characters as gentlemen by virtue of their
conduct, not their rank or riches, Pinero emphasized that individual worth—not labels, or appearances, or conformity to a code—
ought to be prized. Without the influence of Ibsen, he had on his
own become interested in the falsity of appearance, the shock of
disillusionment, and the desirability of facing reality. Perhaps in-
fluenced by Dumas *fils*,[21] he began to deal with the past as a cause
for the present.

If Pinero's early plays seem tentative in their experimentation,
the explanation lies partly in certain theatrical conditions of the
times. The presence of the conventional characters who seem so
out of place alongside more original ones arose from demands of
the prevalent acting style. Characterization in the drama had to
be tailored, to some extent, for actors trained in the then obsoles-
cent stock-company system. The dramatist used the talents of
actors who were experienced in certain types of roles. The creation of vastly original characters would have been to no purpose if

the actors could not create them. Furthermore, plays had to make
an immediate mark in the theater, for the author could not count
on royalties from either publication or movie rights to make up for
losses on a merely artistic success. Out of necessity, Pinero made
his debut as a man of the theater writing for success in the
theater. Later, when he was financially secure and when audiences had been properly tutored to accept changed conditions, he
could strike out in a more independent direction. At this point, he
could not really develop any faster in the way that his talent led
him—toward Realistic character drawing.

CHAPTER 3

Farceur Extraordinary

FOR centuries farces had used lively incidents of an intrigue to govern stock characters rigidly. Shorthand characterization, relying on such devices as tics, laughably exaggerated physical traits, eccentric language, or personanyms (tag names for characters suggesting their traits), sufficed. Such characters did not need the depth of portrayal that results from showing them as decision-making, intelligent creatures; for they were largely automata in a contrived situation, the foremost ingredient of farce. This scheme had served as the framework for plays by most great comic playwrights, and it underlay the Gilbert and Sullivan operas and Wilde's *The Importance of Being Earnest*. That it should have appealed so strongly to the earnest Victorians is a little puzzling, unless one assumes that this highly theatrical genre afforded them an escape from their rigidly proper and decorous lives. A more adequate explanation is given by Eric Bentley, who has said that farce satisfies the usually repressed urge to violate the sanctity—or supposed sanctity—of some institution or assumption.[1]

Capitalizing on the popularity of farcical plays in the early 1880s, young Pinero modestly set out "to raise farce a little" from its "low pantomime level." He treated it "upon lines as artistic as possible, thinking . . . that farce should have as substantial and reasonable a backbone as a serious play."[2] His predilection for drawing believable characters led him eventually to discard the old stock figures and to create roles that were more than vehicles to exhibit a single actor's talents. Drawing upon the wealth of types in Victorian society, he grounded his plays in observable Victorian realities and created fresh emblems of the institutions and assumptions whose sanctity his audiences may have secretly wanted to violate. The result was a new formula for farce based on showing possible people doing improbable things.[3]

I   The Rocket

Pinero's first full-scale venture into the realm of farce was a
"clever but trivial piece of Thackerayan comedy," [4] *The Rocket*
(1883), whose title evidently signifies "one who is going up in the
world." He composed it especially for Edward Terry, an excellent
"eccentric comedian" who met enthusiastic response in the title
role,[5] that of a coarse pretender and flattering parasite, the Che-
valier Walkinshaw. Traveling about Europe masquerading as the
father of the girl Florence, Walkinshaw hopes to find her a husband who, like a good Stilton cheese, will be rich and mild; for,
when his ward marries "coin," his status will rise like a rocket. Secretly overjoyed to find young Joslyn Hammersmith, he nevertheless affects dissatisfaction with his qualifications and only reluc-
tantly accepts him as a son-in-law. Thus, with the engagement
arranged in the first act, the plot cannot focus on a love chase;
instead, true to its satiric intention, it moves on toward the unmasking of the parasite-hypocrite.

In the second act, Walkinshaw proceeds to install himself, Tar-
tuffe-like, in Lady Hammersmith's home, posing as her admirer.
Joslyn, mindful of Florence's tender feelings, hesitates to turn out
his future father-in-law; but he does want to save his mother from
disgrace. Florence, who is aware of Walkinshaw's hypocrisy, as
well as of his buffoonish malapropisms and pretentious meta-
phors, and who appreciates Joslyn's dilemma, quietly slips away
to Paris. For one reason or another, all the other characters also
decide to go there; and in the third act, when on their way to the
Continent, they independently arrive at a Folkestone hotel, where
they are maneuvered awkwardly in and out of their hiding places
in adjoining rooms until the long-delayed recognitions and denouement.

Florence is revealed to be the daughter of a pathetic character
who had left her years ago with his brother (Walkinshaw) when
he was leaving for India and who has been seeking her throughout the play. Walkinshaw is also revealed to be a husband already; thus Lady Hammersmith must quickly forget her infatua-
tion for him. When "The Rocket" has "come down like a stick," he
is expected to apologize. Unexpectedly, he maintains that he has
nothing to be ashamed of; he has only been trying to provide for
himself in old age. As a result he has given Joslyn a wife; taught

Lady Hammersmith a lesson; prevented a foppish character, Lord Leadenhall, from forming a misalliance (with Walkinshaw's wife, Rosaline); and returned Florence to her father. Audaciously, he asks the audience for applause in a speech worthy of Doolittle in Shaw's *Pygmalion*. Pinero's buffoon, who remains unchastened, exists as a device character precisely to do all the things that he has enumerated. His unmasking thus backfires, in a sense, and the satire evaporates when the audience is playfully asked to applaud his expedient rascality rather than the removal of his "comic flaw" or eccentricity.

Aside from the unexpected ending, the play has topical freshness. In no earlier play did Pinero make so many allusions to the current scene. Principally these center on Lord Leadenhall, who complains that he and his friends are being "hit off" in satirical magazines like *Punch*, which he thinks should be barred from any respectable house. He is described in stage directions as a "fair youth of the Masher Type, foppish and affected"; and he speaks of one of his friends who went on the stage and was forced to "play a Masher in a nasty Opera Bouffe," perhaps an allusion to Gilbert and Sullivan's *Patience* (1881). These topical references do nothing to advance the plot, but they show Pinero becoming conscious of the manners of the age.

II In Chancery

By 1884, farcical stereotypes and conventions had become so tiresome to Pinero that he could parody them for his growing public in *In Chancery*, another hit featuring Edward Terry. The title, implying both proceedings in litigation and a hopeless predicament, stresses, as is appropriate in a farce, situation rather than character. The central character loses his memory in a railway accident and narrowly avoids committing bigamy before he regains it. Following the rule of three already tried in *Girls and Boys*, three mysteries are exposed and solved: that of the identity of the amnesia victim, that of the identity of a couple traveling as lady and serving-man, and that of the hotel proprietor's health. (Everyone pampers this irate Irishman by never crossing his wishes; for, if he should get excited, a bullet supposedly lodged inside his body might at any moment cause his death.) In addition, through lavish use of coincidences, three romances are safely concluded by the play's end: the amnesiac, Marmaduke Jackson,

is restored to his "widow"; the lady and her "man" are revealed to
be man and wife; and the Irish girl who nearly married Jackson
gets her father's doctor instead.

Although *In Chancery* was called a "comedy" when it was licensed by the Lord Chamberlain, a traditional farce by Clayton
Hamilton,[6] and a fantastic comedy in French's acting edition, the
excessive staginess of the play makes it a parody of the conventional farce. The characters are described and introduced in by far
the most clichéd manner of all these early plays: one is fat, red-
faced, bushy-haired, and gruff-voiced; his companion is thin, bald,
and shrill-voiced; the detective has a "sharp, enquiring manner";
the serving-man is tall, fair, slim. The hero has fair hair, roving
eyes, a large forehead, and a pale, anxious face. The hotel owner,
whose "humour" is irascibility, has a fiery face, red whiskers, and
bushy hair; and he and his daughter are stage Irishmen—Pinero's
first. The virtue of such stereotyped characters is that they behave
as expected in contrived farcical situations. But the excessive ob-
viousness of Pinero's simple, bold-line method of drawing them
implies parody.

Similarly stereotyped is some of the strategy employed. When
the curtain rises, some regular patrons of the hotel barroom are
asking the Doctor to explain to them about McCafferty's long-
standing illness, "if it's not a secret." One character, who needs to
divulge some exposition, approaches the Doctor and says, "I've
been longing for a confidant." "Mysterious and melodramatic"
music is specified, as well as Mendelssohn's "Wedding March"
and "Home Sweet Home." Soft music accompanies the rise of
each act's curtain, and it is heard repeatedly as the background
for soliloquies or confessions. In Act Two there is a clever escape
scene: Jackson lowers himself from an unseen window on the
floor above past the window of the locked room in which most of
the other characters are melodramatically crying for help. Finally,
a photograph of the actor playing Jackson is the clue for revelation of his identity. On the whole, these effects mock a style of
playwriting which they also partake of. The diction occasionally
bursts into a fairly good line like McCafferty's "Begorra! it's not
bigamy, but trigonometry, he's been attempting." Archer's rank-
ing the play among the "neatest and finest pieces of humorous
workmanship" on the modern stage[7] seems excessive unless he
also considered it as a parody.

III   The Magistrate—*a Masterpiece*

The successes of Edward Terry in both *The Rocket* and *In Chancery* evidently convinced Pinero that farces were what audiences wanted. Responding to an appeal in late 1884 from John Clayton and Arthur Cecil, co-managers of the Court Theatre since 1881, he undertook to write a popular farce for them. He is said to have persuaded them to fill their bills with farces and light comedy; and, when they inaugurated this new program, their theater attained a sound financial footing for the first time. With his *The Magistrate*, they broke records for long-running plays by presenting over three hundred performances after March, 1885.[8]

The Magistrate is Pincro's first masterpiece, and it well exemplifies his formula for sophisticated farce. It maneuvers a dignified Victorian magistrate, Aeneas Posket, through a succession of possible improbabilities toward the comic indignity of very nearly being brought to trial in his own courtroom. His anomalous position is caused by no comic flaw in his character; for this upright judge and idealistic practical philanthropist has been deceived by his newly acquired second wife. She has shaved five years off her age and that of her nineteen-year-old son. The judge's attempt to play the role of firm, protective, but understanding stepfather to this precocious young gentleman who passes for fourteen originates his comic troubles.

Initially, Mrs. Posket, realizing that an old friend of hers is likely to make some unlucky allusion to her son's christening at the next evening's dinner party, attempts to keep her deception unknown and begins another intrigue. With her sister Charlotte, she searches for her friend, Colonel Lukyn, to warn him; and, in the process, she once again deceives her spouse by telling him that she must visit a sick friend. When she has left, her son Cis invites Posket to supper at the hotel where he has kept a room for the entertainment of his young friends. Posket both does not want to deceive his wife about going out and hesitates to be so unconventional as to take supper outside the home late at night. These good intentions clash with his desire to be a good stepfather; but he goes, intending, as he says, to put an end to the young scamp's excesses.

By zany coincidence, Colonel Lukyn and his friend, Captain Vale (lately engaged to Charlotte), have decided to sup, for old

time's sake, in the room which Posket and Cis have occupied.
When Posket and Cis have obligingly taken the next room, the
Colonel receives Posket's wife and sister-in-law, while Vale waits
on a balcony outside. Because Charlotte has had no food on her
day's journey, she, at Lukyn's merely polite invitation, devours
much of the men's supper. When Vale steps back into the room,
there is a lovers' quarrel; and it is prolonged beyond the official
time for closing the public rooms. Dutiful policemen of Posket's
own bailiwick raid the establishment, and all six characters hide in
the same room. When an astute inspector detects their presence in
the darkened room by sounds of breathing, Posket and Cis manage to escape, without learning who the others were with whom
they had hidden in the dark.

The next morning the sedate magistrate appears in his ante-
chamber disheveled after his night of flight. Not having been
home, he worries about having deceived his wife; for he is unaware that she is about to appear before him in court. Lukyn,
obtaining special permission to speak to him, begs him to allow
the ladies to go unquestioned; but Posket, valuing impartiality in
justice, denies the chivalrous request. In the courtroom, off-stage,
he almost goes berserk when he realizes who the prisoners are and
metes out a far too heavy sentence, forgetting his own complicity
in keeping the supper rooms open after hours. Later, matters are
righted by Bullamy, Posket's partner; he rationalizes that, since
the young gentleman had kept a room at the hotel, the others
could technically be considered his guests; therefore, no legal vio-
lation had occurred. Mrs. Posket finally confesses her original
deception; but, with great verbal dexterity, she puts the best possible coloring on it. Lacking woman's commonest fault, exaggeration, she says, she did not want to compete with her husband on
the question of age; hence, she had added to his advantage by
subtracting from her years. Cis, on discovering that he is actually
nineteen, begins seriously to consider marrying Beatie Tomlinson,
his young piano teacher who loves him so much that she has on
this particular day appeared for the music lesson five hours early.
Eager to be rid of the viper Cis, who has corrupted him and stolen
his marital bliss, Posket promises to give Cis a thousand pounds to
marry and start immediately for Canada. By expressing his strong
aversion to the youth so unashamedly, he steps out of the role
enjoined upon him by his public dignity. This quick and pleas-

antly surprising ending goes slightly, however, beyond the actual termination of the complications. In the two small subplots, which do graceful service to the major plot, Charlotte and Captain Vale return to affectionate terms again; and the happy ending of their quarrel and of Cis's and Beatie's romance helps to restore domestic quiet at the Poskets' home.

Most of the characters experience some inner conflict and have more depth than farce ordinarily requires. Posket, presumably honorable in every way, must become an actual fugitive from the law which he himself represents; his role as upholder of the law does not accord with his role either as father or as fugitive. Agatha Posket is torn between her desire to be truthful and her fear of disclosure. When she must behave unconventionally, she invents a conventional reason for doing so. Cis's almost adult instincts cause him to behave in a way which ill befits a supposed fourteen-year-old boy. Beatie tries to behave as a "proper" young lady and also to bespeak her affection; she pretends to be teaching him piano lessons in order to be near him. Charlotte knows decorum; but, being ravenously hungry, she behaves unlike a lady. Colonel Lukyn, an amusing soldier given to sentiment, agonizes over Vale's being drenched outside on the balcony; but he cannot break his promise to the ladies that the three of them could be alone. His role as host and his role as friend conflict. Though Bullamy, whose "humour" is excessive love of jujubes, appears more conventionally drawn, he too has a slight struggle: he preserves the dignity of the law by twisting it slightly to mask the indignity of his friend's wife and sister-in-law. Formerly he has seemed impartial like Posket.

In almost all these instances, strong contrast develops between the inner and the outer lives of the characters, a contrast which considerably enriches this delightful farce. The perfectly adequate soliloquies and asides evoke this contrast nicely. Archer praised the play in 1886 as a "quite masterful" piece of fantasy and as a product of inventive humor on a heroic scale; and he also noted with favor how skillfully Pinero managed to "exclude offence" in the story of a magistrate, one of the symbols of Victorian society.[9]

IV   The Schoolmistress

After this initial triumph, Pinero supplied the Court Theatre with other exceptionally successful farces, even after Clayton's

death and a change in the management. The next one was *The
Schoolmistress*, which opened in March, 1886, and ran until January, 1887.[10] Here Pinero portrayed another title figure symbolic of
Victorian propriety and developed more fully the idea of people
in real life playing roles, their true selves disguised.

From rapid exposition through servants' talk, the audience
learns that Miss Constance Dyott, principal of Volumnia College
for Daughters of Gentlemen, is mysteriously going away for a
month or so at Christmas vacation. Of the four girls being left
behind, one, Dinah Rankling, especially needs watching, as her
parents think that she has "been fallin' in love or something, and
has got to be locked up." The other girls have offered to help
Dinah defy her parents and join her secret husband of three
weeks, Reginald Paulover. Miss Dyott also has just been secretly
married to Vere Queckett, a penurious gentleman of fashion, who
has planned to give a party for his friends while she is gone. Discovering his plans, the girls threaten him with disclosure if he will
not let them combine his party with theirs celebrating Dinah's
marriage. He agrees to play the role of their uncle. The audience
also learns that Miss Dyott, unable openly to acknowledge her
role as wife because to her husband's family she would appear
beneath him, is equally unable to reveal her true plans for the
vacation: she is abdicating her schoolmistress position long
enough to appear in a comic opera. Here the role-playing attains
complexity on several levels: Mrs. Queckett, still pretending to be
Miss Dyott in real life, takes the assumed name of Constance
Delaporte, in order to enact the role of Queen Honorine in the
comic opera. She undertakes this slightly disreputable action in
order to earn more money for her husband's extravagances, having up to now kept him on a strict allowance. As she says good-
bye, she leaves money for rent, servants' wages, and fire insurance.

In the second act, the party, which has nearly consumed the
household money, affords hilarity. The feast, a symbol of revolt
against all the conventions (Dinah's against parental authority,
the other girls' against Miss Dyott's, Vere's against his wife's, the
male guests' against their soberer roles), turns out to be a grave
disappointment: the lark pudding is "architecturally dispropor-
tionate" to the number of guests, and the oysters are suspected of
being "inland oysters" (it has been "a long time since they had a

fortnight at the seaside"). Once again, the metaphor of unsatisfactory food explains frustration. Furthermore, Admiral Rankling, who by coincidence is included among the guests, is obviously disturbed by the presence of the wedding cake. Unhappy in marriage, he is even oblivious of his own daughter's identity; and it is as if he rejected a father's role. Dinah's young husband, who is a "humours" character in his possessive jealousy of his new wife, quarrels with the other men and spoils the fun. Finally, the off-stage antics of a servant—he is shooting fireworks—set the school on fire, an eventuality prepared for by his comment in Act One: "Friction is the risk I run." Vere dispatches insurance money to the nearest mailbox; and while hosts and guests wait to be led out the window, two preposterous firemen amuse them with stories. In a spectacular ending, Miss Dyott reappears, symbolically wearing her costume as Queen Honorine, and rescues her husband.

Curiously, no mention of the insurance occurs in the final act, suggesting that the real problem of this farce is what happens to the characters. In an ordinary farce, the fate of the school would be paramount, and the status quo at Volumnia College would be restored. But in this honest ending, nothing can change Mrs. Reginald Paulover back into Miss Dinah Rankling, or restore the innocence of the schoolgirls, who had supposedly not known of the existence of lobster salad and champagne. The title character undergoes the most profound change: Miss Dyott becomes extinct (hence the question about the school is irrelevant), and her alter ego, the actress Constance Delaporte, is granted life through her smashing success. By daring to be unconventional (and comic in a role which ill assorts with her dignity), she only figuratively commits suicide. She thus finds new life for herself and her husband and a role which she is better fitted to play. Queckett, who has begun to think his marriage injudicious, approves the change, especially since during the promised long run of the opera his actress-wife stands to earn fifty pounds a week. In the curtain speech, Pinero brings play and life closer together when he allows the actress to turn to her real audience and say, "I hope none will regret the change—I shall not, for one, while the generous public allow me to remain a Favourite!" He elicits the audience's tacit approval of the schoolmistress's becoming an actress, as well as her still more anomalous position (in the Victorian era) as bread-winner.

One critic, writing in 1905, praised Pinero's skill in working out his theme, which he described as the futility of keeping a young couple apart and the weakness of trying to "cover up a social position."[11] But the more comprehensive theme is rebellion against the code of respectability in Victorian society, and its various consequences, none of them catastrophic. Even at this point, Pinero did not unquestioningly accept the rigid code of Victorian propriety.

V Dandy Dick

When *The Schoolmistress* was nearing the end of its run, Pinero became dissatisfied with the two acts of a play which he had been composing to take its place and made an entirely new beginning. In record time he developed his idea into three acts and readied the play, *Dandy Dick*, for an opening in January, 1887.[12] The title is the name of a race horse which brings woe to the Very Reverend Augustin Jedd, Dean of St. Marvells Church. The Dean is plagued at the outset by typical Pineroesque concerns: financial difficulties, arising from his flighty daughters' interest in fashionable clothes and his own generosity in a fund-raising campaign to restore the minster spire; and reputation, the dignity of his deanery being threatened by the reception into his household of Georgiana Tidman, his sportswoman sister, who has part ownership of Dandy Dick.

Eventually, the Dean's need for money leads him to abandon his principles to the extent of allowing his servant to place a bet for him. To insure the safety of the horse (and his chances of winning), the Dean goes out to the stable during the night to give the horse medicine and is arrested for attempting to poison it. His dignity has certainly deserted him when he must be rescued by his sister from the local constabulary. He is saved from total disgrace by the constable's failure to recognize him and by his own failure to profit from betting: his servant in error has bet on the losing horse. He finally acquires a thousand pounds to donate to the restoration fund from his sister, who has won heavily in the races.

This main story line affords considerable genuine humor; and it is not precisely farcical since the broad actions that would afford most uproarious laughter, such as the Dean's rescue, are not shown on stage. Much more than in ordinary farces, the leading

character struggles against his fate, resisting the dramatist's maneuvers with a life of his own. In the inward struggle which precedes each successive step of inevitable involvement, the Dean
reveals his humanity. Outwardly, he is the dignified Dean, who
does not play cards in the deanery, is firmly against betting on
principle, and does not speak a slighting word of anybody. Beneath this façade, he is the remnant of the young man who used
to love horses and sporting events while at Oxford; he genially
detests one of the two young men who come to call on his daughters; and, as a tortured man in financial difficulties, he indulges,
just this once, in a bit of innocent immorality in the interest of a
worthwhile cause. Because he has lived the role of a dean so long
that he has almost become an automaton, his re-humanization
affords delight, especially through the irony inherent in his being
rescued by his "disreputable" sister and her racing friends. At the
end, the Dean laments that "the genial summer of the Deanery"
has been "frosted by the winter of Deceit"; but he is considerably
more human.

The lesser complications involve mainly the two daughters,
who have unusual names for a dean's offspring—Salome and
Sheba. Though six years apart in age, they have quite similar
tastes and foibles: love of finery, impracticality except in the
matter of planning to escape to the ball, waggishness, and vitality
enough to torment the most patient father. Their beaux, caricatured as fools, possess the very human attributes of jealousy,
desire for attention, and susceptibility to the young ladies' charms.
They are also somewhat akin to "humours" characters: Major
Tarver in his hypochondria and almost manic-depressive moods
(attributed to his giving part of his liver in service to the Queen in
India), and Lieutenant Darbey in his rude, patronizing self-
centeredness. The courtships are stylized late Victorian ones in
what has been called a "Trollopian home," [13] but no hint of sentimentality intrudes in the treatment of courtship. Indeed, the success of both romances gives the good Dean an unconventional
reason to rejoice—he will now be relieved of the girls' extravagances.

The third love affair in *Dandy Dick* is that between Georgiana
Tidman, *née* Jedd, and Sir Tristram Mardon; and their mature,
sensible match is a contrast to the romances of the young "fillies."
The widow Tidman's entrance is skillfully prepared for by Dean

Jedd's telling his daughters of her plan to come to live with them. He leads them—and the audience—to expect a "sad, broken creature . . . a wave-tossed derelict." But, when she appears, her racing jargon and her hearty manner typify anything but a "weary fragment." Her first comment to him and his reply effectively contrast their styles both of talking and living:

> GEORGIANA: Well, Augustin, my boy, it's nearly twenty years since you and I munched our corn together.
> THE DEAN: Our estrangement has been painfully prolonged. (p. 14)

She continues using stable phraseology throughout the play just as he maintains his ecclesiastical stiffness. When fire breaks out at the local inn, she rushes impulsively to save Dandy Dick, whose ownership she shares with Mardon. When her unconventional mannish behavior and control give way to an impulsive show of emotion over the horse's burnt tail, she wins Mardon's affection.

On the whole, the pace is swift, rising in the first act to Georgiana's upsetting suggestion that her nieces bet on a horse; in the second, to the revelation that the Dean has been arrested; in the third, to anticipation of failure to rescue the Dean from the constable's cart, and finally to the swift arrangements for matrimony and the other resolutions. The play is so tightly constructed that any incident in the major plot affects the subplots and most of the characters. For instance, the fire at the local inn burns the inn stables and occasions the bringing of Dandy Dick into the deanery stables; and it also dashes the hopes of the Dean's daughters for a romantic escapade at the fancy-dress ball since their two lovers are recruited into the fire brigade and the ball is canceled. The fire also brings the Dean's sister close to his old friend, Mardon. Even Dean Jedd's ill-fated attempt to administer a bolus to the horse results in more than his mistaken imprisonment: it affords the servant Blore grounds for comic blackmail; and, by giving the girls a false impression, it leads to their setting out in married life to avoid their father's "evil" influence, or so they rationalize.

Even the minor characters are interesting. The excellent comic butler, Blore, is a descendant of the intriguing servant in ancient comedy. Noah Topping is a gruff, conscientious constable obsessed by jealousy of his new wife, Hannah; he was modeled after an actual minor magistrate in a village near Brighton, where Pinero wrote the play.[14] The humanity of the characters extends even to Hannah, the cook, who has recently married Noah after serving the deanery for seven years. Considering that she owes more allegiance to her former employer than to her constable spouse, she undertakes to deprive her own husband of a prisoner. These individuals are by no means stereotyped "low" characters.

But the most impressive achievement of the play is the consistent sprightliness of its dialogue and the appropriateness of each variety of diction to character. The girls' vivacity is immediately apparent in the opening scene from a tongue-in-cheek argument between them. Their aunt's language nonplusses them most of all; when she tells them to put their "very petticoats" on Dandy Dick, their shock in misunderstanding brings down the curtain on the first act. The Dean's euphemistic speeches can bring no charge of artificiality on the playwright, for they are entirely in keeping with the character's stuffiness. In Act One, reprimanding the girls for extravagance, he intones: "Your dressmaker's bill is shocking; your milliner gives an analytical record of the feverish beatings of the hot pulse of fashion; your general draper blows a rancorous blast which would bring dismay to the stoutest heart. Let me for once peal out a deep paternal bass to your childish treble and say emphatically—I've had enough of it!" When asked whether he is hungry, after a night in jail and no breakfast, even though he smells a tempting meal being cooked, he can reply, "I am sorely tried by your domestic preparations."

In the asides, Pinero again conveys a sense of the inner lives of his characters, especially in an interesting passage in Act Two, which takes place after a dull and disappointing dinner. Sitting in the parlor, six characters in one aside after another reveal their preoccupations. The girls think aloud about their dresses and their planned escape to the ball; Major Tarver expresses his hatred for Lieutenant Darbey, who has thrown the Major's music out of the carriage, thus making it impossible for him to sing; and Darbey, while playing the violin, glories in his triumph. Meanwhile, the Dean worries about financial difficulties; and Georgiana considers how to place her bets the next day. She has the most objectivity in that she surveys the scene with some amusement and distaste and says, "No—there's nothing like it in any other country. A regular, pure, simple, English Evening at Home!"

Dandy Dick has enjoyed a greater number of revivals than most of Pinero's plays. With its sophisticated modern variations of conventional farcical concerns, its pleasingly fresh characters, and its clever dialogue, it has proved its ability to amuse audiences.

VI   The Cabinet Minister

After Pinero had embarked on a new career as author of serious problem plays, he still retained his firm hold on the technique of farce. As he confessed, he customarily rested from the labor of writing a serious play by composing a farce.[15] In writing *The Cabinet Minister* (1890) soon after his first true problem play, he rested by attacking the dignity of another upright Victorian type and pleased his old audience at a new Court Theatre. The production made an auspicious beginning for the new venture.

The Cabinet Minister is a thickly populated, diffuse play with many story lines. One story concerns a young married couple who quarrel periodically over the career which their infant son should pursue; their outrageousness disappears when finally they agree not to disagree. Another concerns ridiculous attempts to arrange a match between Sir Colin Macphail, a Scots nobleman who is a "mama's boy," and Imogene Twombley, daughter of the cabinet minister. This match grows into a complicated double triangle when Mrs. Gaylustre, a dressmaker who poses in the evenings as a person in society, uses feminine wiles to rouse the Scotsman's affections and when Imogene realizes that she prefers the company of her reclusive unconventional cousin, Valentine White, to that of the Scot. Another love story features a foppish young man, Brooke Twombley, who courts his cousin Euphemia in the modern unimpassioned, understated way. There is also the story of a crass money lender, Joseph Lebanon, brother of Mrs. Gaylustre, who makes bold and ridiculous moves to be received into society; he is the comic villain, whose harsh thwarting, however, at the end seems undeserved.

The major story details the domestic affairs of Lord Julian Twombley, the cabinet minister, and Lady Kitty. Exaggerated sentiment is the keynote of her character. Of very humble origin herself, she wants her children Imogene and Brooke to be well provided for before she and her husband retire to the country to grow their own vegetables, as he often threatens to do. She wants Imogene to marry Sir Colin Macphail, and she must of necessity pay for her overindulged son's wild extravagances. Also unable to curb her own expenses, she has grave financial difficulties. Lebanon, in return for vast loans, wants an entrée into society, as well as information about cabinet decisions which will allow him to make a fortune in stock-market speculations. Pressed by him, she fails in the crisis and steals into Sir Julian's study to learn a cabinet decision concerning a canal project, which the steadfast Sir Julian would never disclose, even to her. Happily, however, Sir Julian has overheard them and scribbled a misleading note on the basis of which Lebanon presumably bankrupts himself. Realizing that the true cabinet decision will be the obverse, Lady Kitty then speculates with her nephew's money and solves her financial problems. Sir Julian, of course, is innocent of any intent to use his knowledge fraudulently; but he resigns anyway. At the end, Lady Kitty resolves to be wise—tomorrow.

The characters, though far more varied than usual, are drawn in a more obviously formulaic way. Sir Julian, the title character, who is by no means the central figure, is shadowy and dim compared to the highly detailed portrait of Judge Posket or Dean Jedd; but Sir Julian is, like them, an idealistic man. Tricks of diction sketch Brooke Twombley, who ends most of his statements with a mildly exclamatory "What!" and also the Dowager Countess of Drumdurris, who always "has a motive." Lord Macphail's taciturnity is his main trait. Valentine White, who dresses in an outlandishly informal way to show his contempt for social forms, dons traditional clothing when he realizes that he can have the love of the lively, fresh Imogene. Aside from Lebanon's moneylender's cant, he is characterized by his difficulty in making polite conversation and by one droll attempt to tell a self-centered story to a gradually disappearing audience. His characterization as social climber would be appropriate to a comedy of manners.

From the general effect, one receives the impression that, by creating a bustling scene, Pinero was trying hard not to repeat himself. The nearly frenzied atmosphere indicates the milieu that two characters within the play, Sir Julian and Val White, wish to escape; but it also represents the author's manifest attempt to escape not only repetition in the farcical realm but also the pressures of composing problem plays.

VII   The Amazons

After completing *The Second Mrs. Tanqueray* in 1892, Pinero indulged in his characteristic relaxation by writing his last farce for the Court Theatre, *The Amazons,* which was actually produced before the problem play. He called it a "farcical romance," but it was received as a commentary on the "new woman." [16] The setting is an imaginary country house called Great Overcote, located in Overcote Park two hours' journey from London. On such a secluded estate the sentimental Marchioness of Castlejordan has pretended for years that her three daughters are sons. Idealistically disregarding reality, she has imposed a comic flaw, disguise, on them; and she has reared them to think, talk, and act like men. They have been coached by a very masculine governess, Sergeant Shuter, in tying fishing flies, in inspecting the Hereford bulls, and in working out in the gymnasium. But, when they go visiting, they wear skirts. Two of the girls, Willy and Tommy (for Wilhelmina and Thomasin), have recently had proposals of marriage while visiting; in the course of the three acts, they are pursued to Overcote Park, wooed, and won. Willy's lover is a stage Frenchman, though he is not characterized by the usual accent; rather, he prides himself on being English in his outlook and in his pronunciation—but he uses grotesquely unidiomatic English. The very masculine Tommy is matched with an effeminate weakling aristocrat, the Earl of Tweenwayes, who can speak only of his hereditary ailments, habits, and prejudices ("We" never smoke, never breakfast, always bring destruction to those we curse, etc.). The third daughter, Noel (for Noeline), has just had an adventure in London: having slipped into town in her male garb, she took part in a street fight to rescue a girl and, fainting, had to be rescued in turn—coincidentally, by her cousin, Lord Litterly, who is the very model of the Anglo-Saxon sportsman and athlete, though a failure at the university. Litterly, having seen through Noel's disguise and fallen in love, enters the park in her pursuit. These three romances constitute subplots which contribute to the denouement in the main plot.

The appropriate reversal comes when, with their mother's permission, the amazons acknowledge their true femininity in the third act. The lovers, trying to keep rendezvous with their ladyloves late at night, mistakenly fall into the gymnasium and hide when they hear the ladies arrive for their usual exercise. Comic contrasts are developed between the girls' lackadaisical exercising and the brisk governess's gymnastic expertise and, when the men come out of hiding, between the girls' submissiveness to Sergeant Shuter and their coquettishness with the men. There follows a standard recognition scene between two persons long separated from each other, Lord Litterly and Sergeant Shuter; for he recognizes her as his nurse of years before. Then in the central reversal, Lady Castlejordan, thought to be in London, surprises them all and confronts Noel with knowledge of her adventure. When Noel confesses and defends herself by alluding to their unusual upbringing, though they are "only weak, chicken-hearted women" after all, Lady Castlejordan acknowledges that nature will have its way by commanding, "Into your frocks! Into your frocks!" When, a little later, she adds that they are never to dress in any other garb, her comic eccentricity has disappeared. The girls re-enter dressed properly, and everybody celebrates at supper the forthcoming weddings.

Pinero expended some ingenuity on the quaint sets. Acts One and Two take place in a clearing called "The Tangle" which features a "ragged hedge," a five-barred gate, a stump of a felled tree, an old tree with a practical wide hollow, and fall foliage; and the whole scene is to be "warmly coloured and poetical in suggestion." Act Three features the "artistically decorated" gymnasium, with skylights, a spacious storage cupboard to accommodate characters who must hide, and such equipment as a vaulting horse, parallel bars, and a horizontal bar.

Some of Pinero's genial satire from *The Times* (see Chapter 5) lingers in this play; but, unlike *The Times, The Amazons* does not wander into a sentimental conclusion. Sentiment is present only in the Marchioness's motive (her disappointment at not having sons) for rearing her daughters unconventionally. Even the projected marriages are not the happy rewards of characters with whom the audience sympathizes, for farcical objectivity rules throughout. *The Amazons* has received high praise for having a gentle strain of poetry running through it; a fresher, more delicate humor and quaint prettiness than *Dandy Dick;* and a clever mingling of romance, comedy, and satire.[17] Fyfe, who says that the play is "founded upon eternal principles of human nature," finds in it "more insight into the heart of things . . . more sympathy with the beating heart of humanity" than in any of Pinero's earlier farces.[18]

VIII   A Wife without a Smile

When, after a dozen years of concentrating on other types of plays, Pinero resumed writing farces, he had lost some of the buoyant mood of the 1880s. Furthermore, his triumphs in other genres had affected his farcical style—so much so that it is difficult to classify the later farces. Specifically, *A Wife without a Smile* (1904), in its emphasis on manners and in its witty diction, resembles a comedy of manners; but it lacks the customary polished, aristocratic characters and is decidedly farcical in the manipulation of the incidents. After it appeared, it encountered charges of vulgarity for its picture of middle-class manners; some critics even wondered why the censor had licensed it.[19] But this comic play with its amoral tone anticipating Somerset Maugham's and Noel Coward's sophisticated naughty pieces would not offend present-day audiences.

The first act introduces the hosts, Mr. and Mrs. Rippingill, and the guests at a weekend party at a country house; and the scene is the comfortably appointed boat-house, where informality can flourish. The guests include a pair of newlyweds, the Webbmarshes; an unattached artist, Vivian Trood; and Mrs. Lovette, a handsome woman of uncertain age. Because Avis Rippingill, who is twenty-one years younger than her husband of two months, has not smiled since their wedding, he rigs up a contraption to make her laugh: a dancing doll suspended, through a hole in the ceiling, from the springs of the sofa upstairs in the Webbmarshes' room. Any pressure on the springs, such as the affectionate newlyweds might exert, causes the doll to dance. This "erotometer" particularly appeals to Rippingill's sense of humor, on which he prides himself; but when it fails to excite Avis's hilarity, Mrs. Lovette and Rippingill take drastic measures. From the ouija board they obtain the answer, Pullinger; so Rippingill sends for his friend, John Pullinger, a ridiculously caricatured owner of cookie bakeries.

In the second act, Pullinger, who proves a mine of such information as where to get the best lead pencils or cheaply dressed dolls for Christmas gifts and where to go in Wales for a honeymoon, advises shock to arouse Avis's "stagnant forces." Rippingill's coincidental discovery that his divorce from his humorless first wife was not valid promises to produce the appropriate shock. However, on hearing that her marriage is illegal, Avis not only sighs with relief and smiles radiantly but laughs and runs out. Rippingill's faint perturbation over his success increases sharply when the doll begins to dance while the Webbmarshes are present. Only Avis and the artist Trood, an acquaintance from before her marriage, are absent.

This ironic reversal is playfully followed in the third act by Avis and Trood announcing their engagement and by Rippingill's and Mrs. Lovette's retaliation: they make good use of the rigged sofa. But, when Avis realizes Trood's prospects of poverty, she rouses herself to rescue Rippingill from the other woman and thereby prevents loss of her own comfortable existence. At the final curtain she is in a position to chide the unsmiling Rippingill for lacking a sense of humor.

Though these events seem to embody Pinero's satiric antagonism for people like Rippingill, the other characters are portrayed with more objectivity. Trood, who as a sincere lover and struggling artist might have evoked Pinero's sympathy, looks ridiculous after Avis's about-face and exits vowing devotion to art as his goddess. Avis makes an obviously expedient rather than romantic choice of a mate. Webbmarsh, having been the butt of mirth-making pranks, will take his revenge by putting his host and fellow guests into a play. By the events in the boat-house he has been inspired, he says, to "hurl, as it were, chunks of raw, bleeding humanity upon the boards" and thereby to revolutionize the drama. One gets the impression that *A Wife without a Smile* is the sort of play such a spiteful playwright would create and that in the coarse fun of the play there is implicit criticism of audiences' tastes.

IX Preserving Mr. Panmure

In the next five years Pinero drew his most telling pictures of British stuffiness, hypocrisy, and materialism in three problem plays; but in two of them a certain amount of farcical exaggeration of unpleasant characters contributes to the effect (see Chapter 6). By the time he again wrote a pure farce, he had become the venerable Sir Arthur; yet in *Preserving Mr. Panmure* (1911) he did not stint his irrepressible merriment.

The play, which continued his attack on sanctimonious hypocrisy, treats in a mock epic fashion the uproar which an innocent
kiss causes in a very proper household, that of St. John Panmure.
Mrs. Panmure has fallen under the spell of the new rector of
Polehampton and is the first member of The Guild of Fine Souls
(or Pruyn's Pure People). Her excess of religiosity, remarked by
at least two other characters, has led her to ban card playing and
to have her husband preach a nightly sermon before guests and
servants. Early in the play, Panmure confides to another character
that he has always been strictly faithful to his wife; but, being at a
loss for material for his nightly sermon and then overjoyed when
Josepha Quarendon, a governess, supplies him with a text, he impulsively kisses her. When the shocked governess pretends to seek
advice for a friend who has been kissed, the other ladies see
through her pretense without guessing the man's identity. The
proper household is immediately scandalized, and Panmure occupies the ironic position of having to lecture the three suspected
guests and urge confession. Finally one of them plays the role of
the rogue and falsely confesses, whereupon Mrs. Panmure nomi-
nates him for membership in The Guild of Fine Souls and pins her
badge on him.

This material occupies three acts. The fourth act, of which two
versions were written,[20] does not follow logically from it; for it
concerns Josepha's choice of a husband. She lets her choice between two men be known in a unique way: she writes "Lucky
Man" on two slips of paper, puts them in a vase, and, by letting
the man who is her own choice draw first, avoids the necessity of
having to refuse the other. A visit from the Panmures and others
who were present at the kissing episode interrupts the proceedings. Panmure, now also extolling the virtues of the rector Pruyn,
has come in order to confess that it was he who kissed Josepha.
He has given up smoking and drinking, but he has also discon-
tinued the sermonettes and will hire new servants to avoid loss of
face. The gravity of his self-abasement contrasts ludicrously with
the slightness of his actual offense.

Hamilton's judgment that the dialogue is brilliant and the
craftsmanship fine seems incontrovertible. The third act, he says,
is a triumph of deft manipulation. But he slights the play needlessly in saying that its merits are mostly technical since Pinero's

ingenuity is employed to develop insubstantial material.²¹ Actually, the play does well what a farce should do.

X *Two Short Plays*

After *Preserving Mr. Panmure,* Pinero wrote only three more farces; and two of them are slight one-act plays. At the St. James's Theatre he presented *Playgoers* in 1912. Like *A Wife without a Smile,* it has implied criticism of audiences and embodies awareness of his own decline in popularity, but without bitterness. The play rests on a simple ironic situation in which servants dominate their masters. A recently married couple, who for eight months have been experiencing servant trouble, seem finally to have employed a perfect lot; and the mistress wants to reward them by sending them in shifts to the theater. Pinero varied the servants' characters as widely as possible for comic contrast and invented a number of variations of their reactions. Then he brought about a strong reversal: both the master and the mistress have lost dignity in approaching the servants with the plan; and, when the latter discover that they are to be sent to see plays with *ideas,* their collective dignity is so offended that they all give notice.

A Seat in the Park, a Warning (1922), the second one-act play, is even slighter. Its action stems from coincidence. A well-dressed gentleman accosts a young woman in the park, very aggressively makes known his interest in her, and begins to wish that he had someone like her at home since his wife does not understand him. As the two prepare to part without arranging any future meeting, she divulges that she is a parlormaid going to a new position on the following Monday—in his home! As the curtain falls, he realizes the ghastliness of his mistake. The only value of the piece is its near parody of the use of coincidence, which Pinero suggested by stipulating that, in staging it, no attempt at realism be made.

XI Child Man

Pinero's last contribution to this genre, *Child Man,* written in 1928, is also difficult to classify, as he admitted in calling it a "sedate farce." Though it emphasizes manners, it lacks aristocratic characters; though it renders a worthy man ridiculous through an entire act, it elicits sympathetic responses for him in a climactic triumph, abandoning the usual farcical objectivity. Perhaps there

is in this play a parallel between Anthony Gillbanks, the historian,
and Pinero, the writer of Realistic plays, as well as between Gillbanks's turning to the writing of children's books and Pinero's ca-
tering to his public in light, inconsequential pieces.

After one act of exposition, in which the scheme for lifting the
Gillbankses out of genteel poverty is planted in Anthony's mind
by his wife Lorna and a painter friend, Colin McCabe, the second
act shows a reversal of their fortunes, which occurs eight years
and a whole series of "Brian and Betty" books later. Anthony, the
"Child Man," has become the idol of children everywhere, though
he detests even his own; and the real Brian and Betty have become monsters of egotism and affectation. They dominate their
childlike father, especially in managing a large birthday party, his
forty-third, for the benefit of prying photographers, newsmen,
and his publicity-seeking admirers and not for his own pleasure.
Their rudeness and his long-dormant sense of betraying his historian's calling bring on his explosion of bad manners. He throws off
his figurative disguise as a child worshiper and turns against wife,
children, friend, and guests.

In the third act, a familiar situation from earlier serious plays—
the near compromise of a woman's reputation—is treated in a de-
lightfully comic and ironic way. McCabe, who has admired Lorna
through the years, thinks that, turned out by Anthony, she is coming to his flat for protection and solace. Delighted, he prepares to
shelter her (and more) and arranges with his landlady to have an
appropriate supper ready. The landlady is a thoroughly fresh
character: by her own admission, she is outwardly "an icicle" but
"inwardly all for vice," and she abets him in his plans to seduce a
married woman because she has come to think that marriage ties
can "go hang." All McCabe's ardor cools rapidly, however, when
Lorna arrives bringing Brian and Betty with her; and the antici-
pated supper becomes the epitome of disappointment.

After a miserable night for all four, McCabe penitently tries to
confess his intentions the next morning to Gillbanks, who arrives
in comfortable old clothes after a restful night and a promising
start on a new history book. That the husband shows no anger or
jealousy but merely scorns McCabe indicates how completely
Pinero and his audiences had departed from Victorian mores.
Gillbanks, who is now concerned only with fidelity to himself and
his art, somewhat too pointedly lectures his "friend" 'about saving

one's immortal (artist's) soul. He also puts the other characters in their places, insisting that Lorna expect a stuffy historian's art to provide for them in the future and that Brian and Betty learn to make themselves useful.

Though the situation returns to normal when McCabe timidly accepts Lorna's invitation to dinner, the play is not merely a pointless farce with a customary ending. It has point in its treatment of two artists who prostitute their talents; and, in its satiric treatment of the publicity seekers and newspaper reporters in the second act, it echoes Pinero's strong distaste for being in the public eye. And *Child Man* would be timely in any era when rude, self-centered youngsters seem to dominate their elders.

XII Assessment

Pinero succeeded in raising farce to a high level. Archer praised *In Chancery* and *The Magistrate* as "more pure-bred" works of art in that they were frankly farces, not indulging in shallow sentiment or pretending to seriousness.[22] The brilliance of the Court Theatre farces easily won recognition in contrast to the style of other plays of the time and called forth the first tributes to Pinero as inventor of a new formula. On the other hand, his achievement in *A Wife without a Smile* and *Preserving Mr. Panmure* paled in comparison with his much more earnest plays and with the drama in vogue after 1900. Hence these two farces and *Child Man,* which has not been produced, have been neglected as totally insubstantial. The only serious technical flaw in the three is the unrelatedness of the final act of *Preserving Mr. Panmure.* All three use irony masterfully, and their anti-middle-class sentiment gives them substance. Adverse criticisms of Pinero's farces probably arise from critics' scorn of the genre rather than from faults of execution in the plays.

In Pinero's development, the farces played an important role. Nicoll says, "Through them Pinero learned the use of his chosen instrument."[23] To the extent that working in this style taught Pinero how to create a convincing air of inevitability, Nicoll is right; but, by 1883, Pinero had already "learned the use of his chosen instrument" when he composed *The Rocket.* In all the farces, the old plot tricks and devices represent the inevitable, certainly; but in *The Magistrate* the characters for the first time have enough credibility to seem to resist the plot maneuvers. They have a past and a future; they have plausible motives; they exist in recognizable contemporary settings. Thus tension develops between plot and character, and the inevitable outcome seems more credible and logical. By imbuing the characters with some reality, Pinero reflected, but theatrically stylized, the actual life and manners of his time. When he turned to the problem play, he imitated plausible events instead of using abstract plot maneuvers; and his characters then came in conflict with the society represented by those events. In this way, the farces prepared for his achievements in the serious plays.

In mapping out his program as farceur, Pinero implicitly criticized theatrical tradition; in the barely submerged irreverence which suffuses the plays, he implicitly criticized the society outside the theater. His critical stance should help to disprove the contention that Pinero always staunchly defended the status quo. Bentley maintains that the Court Theatre farces, along with the Gilbert and Sullivan operas, were the distinctive Victorian contribution to the drama;[24] and Robert Metcalf Smith, by including *The Magistrate* in his anthology *Types of Farce-Comedy* (1928), placed Pinero among a distinguished company of writers: Aristophanes, Plautus, Shakespeare, Molière, John Gay, Gilbert and Sullivan, and Anatole France. The suggestion of Pinero's importance does not seem extravagant. Though Bentley's judgment that the Victorian playwright will be remembered more for these pieces than for any others seems hyperbolic, Pinero must be acknowledged as a master of this sometimes derided dramatic form.

CHAPTER 4

Sentimental Comedist

THOUGH sentimentalism had abounded in English stage comedy since Richard Steele's time, Pinero seems to have come under its spell through fond acquaintance with Robertson's plays and through reading Dickens's novels (as Robertson had done). Not a sentimentalist himself, he used excessive sentiment as a comic foible in some of the farces, notably *The Amazons;* and in some of his earliest comedies of manners he allowed anomalous sentiment to be the keynote of certain aristocratic characters. Gradually he came to realize that audiences still enjoyed indulgence in sentiment for its own sake. As a result, he wrote a series of plays which mingle tears and laughter and which deal with nontragic misadventures of virtuous characters. His success in several of these plays proved his analysis of audiences to be correct and led him to pronounce his age one of sentiment rather than manners.[1]

I Low Water

Pinero's first full-length play to concentrate on sentiment is *Low Water* (1884), an extremely conventional seduction drama in which the seduced heroine is saved in a marriage which reforms her seducer. In three acts, it treats the tribulations of the Linklaters, a rising middle-class family with great expectations of financial and romantic success. The widower-father expects to amass a fortune as a director in a new company, but the firm collapses, and the family undergoes financial reverses. One daughter, Rosamond, nicknamed Beauty, expects to be elevated to the aristocracy through marriage to a nobleman with a significant name, Lord George Ormolu; instead, she is seduced and abandoned.

In subsequent action, considerable irony derives from her father's ignorance of her fate: deceived, he takes false pride in

being allied to a nobleman's house through his daughter. When
the disgraced Rosamond enters again, she meets a forgiving reception, unlike the fallen women in mid-Victorian novels. Her
spirited and loyal sister Anne, despite the family's financial em-
barrassments, refuses to allow Vereker, Lord George's cynical
uncle, to make a monetary settlement of the affair with
Rosamond. Finally, Rosamond wins Lord George's affection by
nursing him faithfully after he has been struck by a carriage. Taking a conveniently sudden turn for the better, both morally and
physically, he controverts his uncle's wishes by marrying beneath
himself socially. The offstage ceremony redeems her reputation
and his ethical sense. Meanwhile, Anne and her beau, Dicky
Smallpage, have come to an understanding also. The curtain line
patently explains, "It is when the tide is lowest that we find the
sunken treasure."

Though this plot is awkward and the story obnoxiously sentimental, Pinero did create for it some interesting characters. Dicky
Smallpage is unusual in combining genial traits with foppishness.
Anne, called the Major, shines briefly in her encounter with
Vereker; by routing him in a defiant, soldierly manner she proves
the aptness of her sobriquet. Vereker has the outlook and sophisticated manners of a Restoration gentleman. But George is drawn
with most depth, perhaps after Dickens's seducers. World-weary,
like Gillian West in *Girls and Boys,* and mistrusting his willpower
to do the right thing, he tells Dicky in Act One that Dicky should
not have saved him from drowning years before. Just as he is going away without Rosamond, she impulsively throws a bouquet at
his feet, a prearranged signal showing her willingness to elope.
This coincidence nullifies his good intentions, though it also leads,
of course, to his redemption at the end.

The mixture of characters—some farcical, some genially humorous, some witty, with others who are sentimentalized or seriously sympathetic—was again painfully awkward in a play which
in other details, especially topical references to contemporary
London, attempted Realism. Archer classed *Low Water* as a failure.[2]

II Sweet Lavender

In several plays written between 1884 and 1886 Pinero infused
sentiment into the basic scheme for comedies of manners (see

Chapter 5); but in late 1886 he began a play,[3] *Sweet Lavender*, which unabashedly evoked the warmhearted, misty-eyed response and which made him wealthy. When he produced it at Terry's Theatre in 1888, he gave Edward Terry his greatest acting success in the role of the genial comic, Dick Phenyl. The play ran for over two years—684 performances, longer than any other Pinero play in its original production—and it had exceptional international success, being translated into German and Italian.[4] The play marks no advance in technique, being imitative of Robertson except in the character of Dick Phenyl. Its happy denouement optimistically answers a Robertsonian query: "Can a young gentleman marry beneath him and expect happiness?"

The story has a background from the actual time of Robertson. In the antecedent action, the banker Wedderburn had a youthful romance with a girl named Ruth, who was beneath him. Declining to form a misalliance with her, he deserted her (as Robertson might have approved); and she went with her illegitimate daughter to London to escape disgrace and settled in the Temple as a "laundress" (landlady). The play takes place fifteen years later in "chambers" shared by Dick Phenyl, a middle-aged lovable tippler, and, by coincidence, Clement Hale, the adopted son of Wedderburn. Clement has fallen in love with Lavender, Ruth's delicate daughter. Through complications which include Wedderburn's near collapse on seeing Ruth again after so many years, the failure of his bank, and Dick's inheriting a large fortune, Clement continues steadfast in his intention to marry Sweet Lavender and finally wins his adoptive father's blessing. Ruth's secret remains safe from Lavender and Clement; and with anticipation of happiness they enter into what would earlier have been considered a misalliance.

This action proceeds according to Pinero's characteristic threefold pattern, for three pairs of lovers are reconciled or betrothed in the play. Aside from Ruth and Wedderburn's reunion and Clement and Lavender's betrothal, a romance blossoms between Minnie Gilfillian, Wedderburn's niece originally attached to Clement, and Horace Bream, Pinero's first American male. At one point, Minnie, who has voluntarily renounced Clement because she sees that he does not reciprocate her love, has an excellent line expressive of her fears of becoming a spinster. Entering a room and discovering tea laid on a table, she says, "Tea! Hot! I must take to tea violently, now I'm going to be an old maid. Tomorrow I'll buy a kitten." When she disregards conventions sufficiently to make her attachment to Bream obvious by throwing a note out the window, she avoids having to become addicted to tea.

The romantic resolutions leave two bachelors unattached. One, the cleverly drawn barber, Mr. Bulger, looks at all the world—even moral problems—exclusively from the tonsorial viewpoint. This "humours" character speaks reproachfully of Phenyl as one who can hardly hold his head up to be shaved twice a week; hence to him Phenyl is "the untidiest chin" in the Temple. When Bulger wants to frighten Ruth Rolt into considering a little more seriously his repeated proposals to her, he enumerates how many throats he has nearly cut and how many wigs he has misfitted through being unable to concentrate on his work for love of her. His main function is to give Ruth a chance to show constancy in her affection for Wedderburn.

The other unmatched male is Dick Phenyl, a Dickensian character somewhat like Newman Noggs in *Nicholas Nickleby*. Instrumental in helping both pairs of lovers, he is, in turn, reformed from tippling by the good efforts of Clement. After seven days of abstinence—a fearful drought, he calls it—he hesitates "even at gravy." He has very humane feelings and undergoes exhausting inner struggles when he finds that he cannot help all his friends at the same time. His dilemmas make him the more lovable, and he becomes the hero.

In an old-fashioned way, Pinero relied on properties like photographs, letters, and newspapers to introduce the complications. His choice of a single stage set as the locale for all the action called for contrivance to make a variety of incidents seem plausible. Hence characters appear and disappear with awkward strategy. Soliloquies and asides make every motive, every disappointment, every hope painfully clear; and the too heavy foreshadowing warns of the impending happy ending.

Sweet Lavender is, in one critic's words, "a comedy suffused with that full-blown indulgence and 'kindly humanity' which we associate with the great novelists of the nineteenth century when they were not in their best vein." [5] Even Pinero spoke slightingly of it later in a letter to Henry Arthur Jones. Differentiating between adapting and merely translating a play for foreign audiences, he said, "They may adapt *Sweet Lavender* till it is sage and onions for all I care. . . ." [6] For his more serious plays, he insisted on direct translation.

III   Lady Bountiful

Pinero's *Lady Bountiful* (1891) so intensifies the pathos that can have a rightful place in sentimental comedy that audiences went away from the theater depressed and saddened, saying that they would not "for worlds" see it again.[7]

Covering nearly seven years, the play traces the romance of the bountiful lady, rich Camilla Brent, and her cousin, Dennis Heron, who accidentally learns of his economic dependence on her in Act One. The discovery impels him to give up his idle, unproductive life (of which Camilla secretly disapproves) and take a job as riding-master in a London academy. Camilla, when she meets him again in Act Two, is so pleased by the change in his character that she proposes to him, though she had ignored his attempt to propose to her earlier. But her reversal is too late: Dennis, thinking that he has caused Margaret Veale, daughter of the academy's proprietor, to fall in love with him, has determined to marry beneath him.

Having managed to put his two lovers as far apart as ever by the end of the second act, Pinero contrived a third act ending in deep pathos and a fourth act catered, finally, to the prejudice in favor of happy endings. Act Three demonstrates Camilla's continuing love despite her disappointment and removes the complication brought on by Dennis's marriage: Margaret nobly exacts Camilla's promise to be Dennis's second wife and then conveniently dies. Though it might seem that now the true loves can be united, Dennis goes away to Nebraska. In the fourth act stagy maneuvers bring him back just in time to save Camilla from a loveless marriage to an older man. At least Pinero refrained from showing their long awaited wedding, in a conventional final scene; but by doing so he further harrowed his audience's already fatigued sensibilities. Throughout the play he seems to have been trying to put his developing Realistic technique to use in bringing about an expected denouement in a novel way.

After reading a few pages in *Lady Bountiful,* one becomes aware of this new note of Realism in managing entrances and exits, in handling exposition, and in finishing scenes and acts. For instance, in Act One the dramatist gives credible exposition by means of characters who are themselves curious; when the information is revealed, he lets them comment on their disappointment that they did not learn much from spying. In Act Two, when he wants to contrive a meeting between Dennis and Camilla at the riding-school, he lets a meddler with a distinct motive bring the two together, intending the meeting to look like an accident, and allows the characters to comment on how strange it is. Again, instead of using a disguise for Dennis in his new role, he merely gives Dennis an assumed name. Instead of using the already overworked situation in which one member of a family really does not recognize another member because of a disguise, he gives Dennis's father good reasons for pretending not to recognize Dennis; namely, a father's proud insistence that his son need not work and his resentment of the son's position as a riding-master because it lowers his own prestige.

But the examples of strong verisimilitude come from the first half of the play. In the last two acts, use of undisguised contrivance blights the effect with an air of unreality. Whereas the first two acts go far beyond *Sweet Lavender* in technique, these last two return to its comforting atmosphere.

Perhaps it was the new Realism, extending into the character portrayals, that, paradoxically, caused the play to fail by dispelling the artificial atmosphere of conventional sentimental plays. *Lady Bountiful* has an abundance of credibly drawn characters, some of them superfluous. Roderick Heron, distinctly the best of the fashionable gentlemen whom Pinero had portrayed up to 1891, has an acknowledged likeness to Harold Skimpole in Dickens's *Bleak House*. He is darkly comic despite his callousness. Camilla's psychology in being both attracted to and annoyed by Dennis is skillfully handled. Dennis develops into a very human character. In a more consistently comic play, his decision to go among commoners would give him the equivalent of a comic anormality; in this play, it is his salvation, giving him contentment and bringing out his best qualities. There are also minor characters who are at once delightful and believable. When Beatrix Brent, a teen-ager who attempts to maintain the fiction that she is "delicate," drops out after Act Two, one is disappointed. The Veales, Margaret's parents, are a credible picture of the lower class rising to middle-class status. Pinero gives all of them understandable motives and appropriate language.

In an inscription printed on the playbill, Pinero insisted on the simple story's lack of offensive matter, perhaps countering charges of offensiveness in his problem play, *The Profligate,* produced two years earlier. He pointed out that the play contained "no war, no lust, not a Commandment broke/By sir or madam . . ." and called it a "history." As a "history," it could be expected to fulfill the Realist's aim of fidelity to actual life; but the absence of any commandment-breakers might suggest both lack of fidelity to life and, to some, lack of interest. As Malcolm Salaman wrote in his introduction to the play, "We are, of course, a very moral and respectable people; but we do not necessarily wish our virtues to be dragged into our amusements." [8] For whatever reason, the play did not have a long run and has not been revived.

IV Trelawney of the "Wells"

In *Sweet Lavender* but much more in *Lady Bountiful,* tone darkens significantly as if both plays unconsciously provided a transition to the problem plays. And both helped Pinero to write one later "drama of real significance," *Trelawney of the "Wells"* (1898).[9]

Trelawney of the "Wells" is one of his most charming and most frequently revived pieces, and in it Pinero achieved absolute mastery of tone. Again, for those who like sentiment there is abundance of it in this story of theatrical people in the 1860s. But the older sentimental style of *Sweet Lavender* is refashioned; the esthetic distance created by period costumes, by the theatrical behavior of the characters when they are not supposed to be acting, by the artistic ideals evinced in their efforts, and by ironic knowledge of the passing of these ideals by 1898 affords an undercurrent of irony. The farcical moments of the play are justified by the fact that those who behave farcically are actors accustomed to acting thus onstage; the earlier farcical style of Pinero contributes to this effect but is also refashioned to fit these more profound character portrayals. And a satirical impulse lies behind the depiction of the non-theatrical characters, who represent the stuffy upper-middle class. Clearly, Pinero sympathizes with his heroine and her associates; and in the plot he brings some of the outsiders around to their way of approaching life. Yet nowhere does sentimentality lead him to overlook the foibles of theatrical folk.

The heroine, Rose Trelawney, because she is about to retire and

begin a new life as wife of Arthur Gower, grandson of stuffy Sir
William Gower, is being honored in Act One at a farewell "cold
collation" by the company of the Bagnigge-Wells Theatre (Sadler's Wells faintly disguised). The setting and action provide the
theatrical folk with opportunities to show their good-heartedness
and their tender regard for one another, as well as their mannerisms, jealousies, and self-centeredness. Even Rose strikes theatrical poses and seems a trifle artificial.

The second act depicts her spiritual trials in the elder Gowers'
household as she yawns away a period of probation before the
wedding actually takes place. Here "the mannerisms and prudish
conventions of the genteel society of Cavendish Square are accen-
tuated to the pitch of burlesque." [10] Just as the torture of her boredom reaches a peak, some of her old friends visit her late at night;
and, because there is a storm, she invites them in, thereby violat-
ing the order and decorum of the heartlessly rigid household.
When Sir William and his sister Trafalgar, aroused from their
beds, scold Rose for entertaining "gypsies," she leaves to resume
her theatrical career. Between the acts, Arthur is presumed to have
left home also to take up an actor's career in Bristol.

Rose's encounter with gentility has had a profound effect on her
when she is seen seven months later in Act Three. She seems to
have lost her ability to act and is on the verge of losing her place
in the company; but she *is* more refined and ladylike. She voices
her new outlook thus:

We are only dolls, partly human, with mechanical limbs that *will* fall
into stagey postures, and heads stuffed with sayings out of rubbishy
plays. It isn't *the* world we live in, merely *a* world—such a queer little
one! I was less than a month in Cavendish Square, and very few
people came there; but they were *real* people—*real!* For a month I
lost the smell of gas and oranges, and the hurry and noise, and the dirt
and the slang, and the clownish joking, at the "Wells." I didn't realize
at the time the change that was going on in me; I didn't realize it till
I came back. And then, by degrees, I discovered what had hap-
pened— (p. 61)

When Sir William comes to her to find out where Arthur is, Rose
cannot tell him because she does not know. Learning that she
tenderly preserves certain mementoes of the great actor Edmund
Kean, with whom her mother had acted, he has awakened within

him old memories of seeing Kean, a "splendid" gypsy; and he softens toward her. Learning also that she is likely to lose her job and that Tom Wrench will use her as the leading lady in his new play if he can find another financial supporter, Sir William penitently, and perhaps too suddenly, offers to back the production. Rose, with her new experience of refinement, will suit the role in the new style of play perfectly since it does not demand the old conventional acting.

Act Four shows a rehearsal of Tom's play, *Life*, some six months later. Sir William, haunted by the reality of one of the characters and by his resemblance to Arthur, who is still missing, begins to regret his earlier good impulse. On the cue for the leading man's entrance, Arthur appears, through Tom Wrench's manipulation, in time to rehearse the role. After the reunion, which further softens and humanizes Sir William, the rehearsal of *Life* resumes. In neither Wrench's nor Pinero's play is there a happy-ever-after ending. With sober restraint, the play called *Life* goes on beyond the final curtain.

The theme of Pinero's play is that the rigid conventions of respectability stifle the heart, but conventions of the theater stifle art. Sir William and Arthur both adjust to Rose's freer manners and learn to live better; but Rose's acting and Tom's writing improve through contact with the Gowers, who live away from the theater with its inbreeding of artificial artistic conventions. But the fact that the theatrical characters elicit more sympathy might seem to suggest the notion that salvation lies in the theater, as Pinero's own success did. The characterization of Arthur Gower parallels Arthur Pinero's own life and beginnings in the theater: his rejection of middle-class surroundings, his apprenticeship in a provincial theater, and his romance with an actress who became his wife. The name of Trafalgar Gower may echo the fact that on his mother's side Pinero was descended from Thomas Wing, who fought at the Battle of Trafalgar.[11] The more natural acting style of Arthur and Rose also reflects the actor Pinero's quiet realism and his avoidance of declamatory effects. Indeed, the playwright acknowledged that scarcely a character in this play was not drawn from his acquaintances in the theater of his youth.

Beyond this autobiographical interest, the play has charm as a semibiographical tribute to Pinero's own hero, Tom Robertson. Possibly the name Tom Wrench suggests the image of wrenching artistic conventions to produce a revolution in style; but, more obviously, Tom "wrenches" events to bring about a happy romantic ending for the lovers in his play, just as he stage-manages life itself by bringing Rose and Arthur together again. He draws characters not from stereotypes but from the people who surround him in Pinero's play. In the fact that a character in Tom's play modeled after Arthur is so "real" that he disturbs Sir William, the line between art and life disappears. Tom's comments also bespeak Robertson's artistic aims, as they echo young Pinero's ideals. He speaks of wanting settings with practical windows and doors placed where they really would be, and he admires the Gowers' drawing room as just the sort that he needs for a play. The title *Life* even echoes Robertson's one-word titles.

In addition to mirroring the manners and low social status of actors in the Robertsonian era, the play records certain other aspects of theatrical history. In it, the theatrical folk sing snatches of actual songs from plays of the 1860s. At the same time that Pinero looks wistfully back on that era, he also effectively parodies the Robertsonian style of dialogue and use of soliloquies in the lines that are rehearsed in the play-within-the-play; and this tension between obsolete and modern dialogue adds charm. And, strikingly, the set for Act Two, the Gowers' drawing room, mocks the ideal of the utterly Realistic box set which observes the "fourth wall" convention: on the upstage wall hangs a (painted) mirror which presumably reflects the fourth wall and its fireplace, which the audience are supposed to be peering through.

V *Three Minor Works*

None of Pinero's plays written during the next twenty years distinctly employ the tears-and-laughter formula, but several evoke the customary feelings of relief and approval by means of fortunate outcomes for sympathetic characters. One of these, *The Widow of Wasdale Head* (1912), is a one-act historical fantasy set in the time of George III. The title character, the widow Jesmond, is proprietress of an estate and an inn. A young guest at the inn, Edward Fane, loves her; but a horrible doubt of her good reputation haunts him since he hears her talking every Friday night to someone in her room. His jealousy and doubt grow upon him until his friend, Sir John Hunslet, likens him to Mr. Garrick playing Othello. Presumably Mrs. Jesmond has been innocently talking to the ghost of her husband, dead for two years. When Hunslet and Fane retire, the apparition enters, accompanied by customary stage effects. Edward, hearing voices, breaks in upon the widow and declares his love when he finds no other substantial person there. But the ghost reappears for Edward to see and frightens him away. Now that his wife has fallen in love with Edward, contrary to her vows and protestations, the ghost begins to fade, illustrating the idea that only her grief for him has given him power to appear to her. She is the typical Pinero heroine, instinctual, warm, and weak. Repenting her inability to be faithful to such an insubstantial lover, she tries to hold him. Grudgingly he forgives her, comparing his feeling for her to what he felt once for his dog; but he fades away beyond recall moments before the curtain falls. Her agitation overcomes her, and Edward and Sir John enter to find her in a faint. The exorcism of the late husband's spirit frees Edward from his suspicions and opens the way to a happy marriage.

The play is of minor interest as a demonstration of Pinero's interest in dialect and in literary history. He drew Edward Fane as a pre-Romantic poet, living in the lake district and inspired by natural beauty; but the lines of Fane's poetry quoted in the play suggest that he has not shaken off the influence of the Neo-Classicists. Though Pinero chose an actual place for the setting, he departed from his usual style to stage the appearance and disappearance of the ghost. When the ghost leaves, the shutters of the inn Expressionistically become transparent.

In another short play, Pinero used domestic sentimental comedy as a framework for propaganda. At the request of the National War Savings Committee, he wrote *Mr. Livermore's Dream, a Lesson in Thrift* in 1915 to encourage saving as part of the austerity program.[12] Briefly, it shows the family of a well-to-do suburbanite quarreling over the question of economy for the war effort. Mr. Livermore selfishly resents any curtailment of his way of life, but his wife Bessie has been encouraging him to practice austerity; and, although the children are cowed by their father, they support their mother's stance. A family friend of long standing, Dr. Appleton, the usual *raisonneur*, reprimands the selfish man and supposedly ruins their friendship. Livermore, dreaming during his afternoon nap, envisions himself as becoming reconciled with his old friend and as being healthier and happier for having espoused economy. When the dream fades, Livermore is shown again as the sluggish, irascible father and husband of the first episode. Only two hours after the quarrel, Dr. Appleton really returns; both men apologize; and, as a result of the dream, Livermore agrees to change his habits. He will give up the car, do the gardening himself, lend the government his savings, eat moderately, and give up smoking.

The play shows further exploitation of Expressionistic technique in representing a dream and in using a transparent setting. The dream episode occupies the middle of the play and affords the actors a challenge to create a contrast with the two "frame" episodes. Otherwise, the play must be called workmanlike propaganda.

In 1918, perhaps to cheer war-weary audiences, Pinero developed the story line for *Monica's Blue Boy*, a ballet-pantomime for which Sir Frederic Cowen composed the music. Such a piece, of course, has no diction and little characterization, and demands simplicity of plot. This one concerns a girl, one of three grown-up children in a suburban middle-class home, who is left alone each day to do the chores for the whole family while the others work in the city. Usually bored with this routine, she suddenly seems to be doing the housework with relish. Noticing her transformation, the others suspiciously arrange to eavesdrop one morning. They discover her meeting a convalescent soldier, wounded during the war, who walks nearby every day; and they learn that the pair want to be married. Their obvious and immediate consternation gives way to joy when the soldier produces evidence that he is of noble birth.

VI The Freaks

A deeper willingness to escape the actual world and straightforward Realism pervades *The Freaks* (1918), and the playwright's bitterness against the self-satisfied new upper class lingers from his most Realistic plays. As in *Trelawney of the "Wells"* two young people change as a result of contact with performing artists. The title ostensibly refers to the circus folk of the play, who are presented sympathetically, though grotesquely; but it also applies to other characters.

An element of fantasy first appears in the indication of the suburban, prewar setting: "those far-off days when, in our ignorance,

small troubles seemed great, and minor matters important." The
device of a will effects the unlikely meeting of the two groups: a
wealthy widow, Mrs. Herrick, owes a duty to a group of freaks in
a sideshow, according to her late brother's will; and, when she
dutifully entertains them at tea, she and her family discover how
vain and quarrelsome the circus people can be.

In the second act, her good intentions have backfired more seriously, for the giant has been confined in her home by illness for
two weeks. Mrs. Herrick's sister and brother-in-law, Sir Norton
and Lady Ball-Jennings, who resent the presence of the friends of
the sick man, complain exaggeratedly of their grossness, their fa-
miliarities, and their lack of respect for aristocracy. On the other
hand, Sheila and Ronald, the young Herrick adults, have fallen in
love: she, with the human skeleton; he, with the contortionist.
However, both are attempting to impose propriety on their lovers.
When all the other freaks gather round the bedside of the worsen-
ing giant and thereby interrupt Sir Norton's attempts to read from
Macbeth, he reveals his own freakish self-dramatization and resentment by refusing to join the vicar and the others in prayers for
the sick man, thinking it sacrilege that prayer should be offered
for such a disreputable person.

On the recovery of the giant in Act Three, the freaks prepare to
leave on a tour of America; and the Ball-Jenningses, having re-
gained the means to move away from the Herrick estate, conde-
scend to see the freaks off and give out souvenirs, but remain ridiculous in their motive: it is to remind the others of their meeting
with Sir Norton and Lady Ball-Jennings. During the sad parting
of the lovers, Ronald and Sheila nearly break down while trying
to hide their regrets. Though Ronald rationalizes that he is glad
that the freaks are gone, Sheila admits that she is glad that they
came.

In this *Idyll of the Suburbs* Pinero wrenches the plot in order to
excite sympathy for the young Herricks, the newer generation,
who will likely benefit from their contact with "splendid gypsies,"
as the author thought he had in his youth. Siding neither with the
grotesque circus characters nor with the caustically drawn pseudo-
aristocrats who are unaware of their own freakishness, he optimistically posits the youngsters' future wholesomeness. In one major
speech, Tilney, the human skeleton, makes the author's point that
the freaks and the spectators ought to change places, an idea

which is also worked out visually: the curtain dropped between the three parts of Act Two has painted on it performing freaks at one side and freakish onlookers at the other, "men and women in evening dress, the men idiotic-looking, the women flashy, *décolletées*, and bejewelled." Perhaps this portrait is of Pinero's increasingly élite audience.

It is pointless to consider whether the love affairs are credible since Pinero obviously stylized them to demonstrate the paradoxical attractiveness of the grotesques. Hamilton, reacting to the bitterness of Pinero's social criticism in the play, suggests that Barrie would have handled the fantasy more purely.[13] Though he is undoubtedly right, the comment is beside the point. Bitterness was definitely part of Pinero's mood; and with some artistry the play says what he meant.

VII   Quick Work

Lacking a text of *Quick Work: A Story of a War Marriage* (1919), a three-act comedy, one must rely on Hamilton's account of it. He had received a prompt copy of the play from Pinero, who called it a slight piece. According to Hamilton, it dealt with a sprightly girl and a war hero who met in January, married in February, and discovered in June that they were "incompatible in temper." Still friends, however, they cheerily set out to establish separate lodgings in preparation for divorcing. Then in a series of psychological changes, which for Hamilton were of major interest, they were reconciled. He called the "narrative material . . . perilously thin," noting that "nothing happens on the stage, except at a single strong moment in the final act." Only four important characters were developed, but these were "studied with meticulous exactitude." The dialogue, he said, was "happily conceived" and seemed natural.[14] Obviously, Pinero was keeping abreast of the new interest in psychology; he deemphasized stage action in order to delve into his characters' minds.

VIII   The Enchanted Cottage

The Enchanged Cottage (1922) has more substance than these other late plays of sentiment. Pinero must have been at work on it as early as 1919, when he wrote Hamilton promising a more substantial play than *Quick Work*.[15] But the death of Lady Pinero interrupted for a time his composition. In 1922 the play had a certain amount of topicality, in that it dealt with a man who has been crippled and disillusioned by World War I; yet it grew out of an even more pronounced mood of fantasy and employed distinctly Expressionistic techniques in developing his theme that love, though blind, is a beautiful regenerating experience.

In Act One, Oliver Bashforth, a crippled war veteran, is living a monk-like life in an old country house when, on a spring day, he is visited by the blind Major Hillgrove and Laura Pennington, a plain woman. Oliver is expecting members of his family to try to persuade him to be less reclusive, or at least to arrange for someone to look after him. The rector of the parish and his wife, farcically exaggerated Dickensian characters, are likely to be asked to supervise his return to "sensible" living. When the pretentious middle-class Smallwoods, Bashforth's mother and stepfather, arrive, they encourage him to "exert himself." To controvert the plans of these officious people, Bashforth offers to marry Laura; and in his proposal he tactlessly argues that he does not need a pretty girl. Laura retorts that even ugly girls have their dreams and that "to spare them too complete an awakening is a deed of charity." Presumably, this arrangement has been promoted by Bashforth's witch-like servant, Mrs. Minnett, who is supposed to have had a witch grandmother.

By the opening of Act Two, Oliver and Laura, now married, have undergone a drastic change. They think of each other as quite beautiful; in fact, Oliver walks without a limp and Laura appears beautiful. The blind Major tells them to accept their transformation as a heaven-sent miracle and encourages them to be sure to scratch their names into the glass of the windowpanes as honeymooners throughout the centuries have done in the old house. After the newlyweds have retired, there is a ballet-like pageant of all such lovers since the time of the Tudors, with music and pantomime of love play. Even children swarm out of the walls. Then Mrs. Minnett appears in the dream as a witch; and the Bashforths' wedding is reenacted, with witch attendants. The vision fades to a tableau of Oliver and Laura sleeping in each other's arms, thereby suggesting that the pageant was their dream.

The third act explains the change in the pair. The Smallwoods are completely baffled since to them Laura and Oliver do not seem to be at all changed. When consulted, Mrs. Minnett explains that their love for each other has made the difference. Laura, left alone at the final curtain, begins dreaming of a baby, whereupon a dream nurse with the face of Mrs. Minnett and the wings of an angel places a baby in her arms.

This dream play suggests that for someone who has been hurt physically as well as emotionally in such an ordeal as war, the only recourse to emotional recovery is retirement to the country, taking solace in the heritage of the past (which the old house represents), and participating in recurrent patterns that human affections create (falling in love, marrying, having children). It repeats Pinero's earlier use of images concerned with sickness, wounds, and disfiguration to suggest that harm comes from too strong devotion to what society demands (see Chapter 6, especially coverage of *The Notorious Mrs. Ebbsmith*). At the same time, its technique visually demonstrates that love—or more literally, imagination—creates beauty. The Major, appropriately blind, can appreciate the magical creation, while the Smallwoods, possessing eyes but lacking both love and imagination, cannot. Though Pinero adopted Expressionism as a controlling device, he did not escape the pitfalls of sentimentality in presenting these ideas. The sentimental tone of the play made it attractive to movie adaptors on two occasions.[16]

IX *Maudlin Sentimentality in a Late Play*

Pinero's last sentimental play, *A Private Room* (1928), is a bathetic one-act piece—an old man's play about two aged lovers, Sir George Darenth and Lady Chinnery. They have dined in the same private dining room at a Soho restaurant every first Monday in July for forty years, except when Sir George was out of the country in service. On the occasion which the play represents, they nostalgically review their past, lamenting that they have not been better spouses to their mates and wishing that they had braved scandal and run away together many years before. Because they cannot count on another year's reunion, he asks whether her husband would permit him to visit in her home; and she says that she will ask. Thus, at a pitifully late stage in life, they attempt to right their earlier errors made through conforming to a code of respectability. They can also look forward, as they opine, to a happy reunion in the afterlife. In this version of elderly love-making Pinero failed to capture the ironic tone which the situation might have suggested to him earlier in his career.

X *Accomplishment*

Pinero wrote sentimental comedy as frequently as other types, but fewer of these creations deserve careful attention. *Sweet Lavender* is important as a reflection of the taste of Victorian audiences, as evidence of Dickens's and Robertson's influence on Pinero, as a contribution to Pinero's early international reputation, and as a great box-office success. Nothing in it promises his later sophistication. That he resisted the temptation to repeat its easy formula does him credit as artist. *Lady Bountiful* affords interest as an attempt to achieve the fullness of the novel and to manage a death scene in what is essentially a comedy. It marks the playwright's advance in technique, but its artistry lapses near the end.

Pinero's crowning achievement in this genre is *Trelawney of the "Wells."* Partaking of a style which it also gently mocks, it can give genuine pleasure to those who see it only as a heart-warming story of two lovers eventually brought together; but, to those who appreciate its irony, it is a subtle and masterful play with more profound implications. Though here Pinero's sentimental reminiscence of his childhood and his theatrical beginnings evoked the rosy world of Robertsonian drama, his ironic commentary properly evaluated the Robertsonian influence and showed Pinero to have surpassed anything that Robertson achieved or undertook.

CHAPTER 5

Chronicler of Manners

FROM the time of Richard Brinsley Sheridan to the end of the nineteenth century few English comedies depicted a *beau monde* with "an amoral approach, witty, clever dialogue, sympathetic characterization, and a certain atmosphere of ease and elegance."[1] For one thing, the aristocracy was no longer such a narrow, stable coterie, since it was being infiltrated from below by merchants, bankers, statesmen, and a few men of letters. For another, the middle class dominated theater audiences and expected to see on the stage images of themselves and of their growing prestige in national life. When playwrights obliged them, plays mirrored "the drab manners or lack of manners of the 'respectable' philistine."[2]

Yet audiences' interest in aristocratic life never entirely ceased. They accepted characters whose sophisticated manners were portrayed as a tasteful expression of individuality, a gesture of pride, or a pathetic relic of the past; they recognized the signs of gentility even as mere exaggeration in dress or carriage. Their bourgeois pride swelled when they saw aristocrats depicted in invidious comparisons with humbler folk. Moreover, they attended numerous revivals of the "old comedy" and applauded the few nineteenth-century plays which approached the manners comedy— notably Boucicault's *London Assurance*, Bulwer-Lytton's *Money*, and certain of Robertson's plays.[3]

Alert to audiences' preferences, Pinero wrote several plays in 1883 and 1884 (especially *Lords and Commons* and *The Ironmaster;* see Chapter 6) in which he depicted snobbish and callous aristocrats changing through confrontations with admirable, earnest characters from the lower classes. But because he was charmed by the bright, sophisticated characters of manners comedies in which he had acted, he began also to depict the upper class in an almost entirely favorable way and to direct his satire against certain figures from the middle class.

I The Weaker Sex

The Weaker Sex, completed in the winter of 1884, began as a comedy of manners about sophisticated upper-class characters who are nevertheless capable of genuine sentiment and in its original ending gratified the audience's romantic feelings while it also presented the pathos of a mother's renunciation. The play had to wait almost four years for a production because, when he showed his draft to John Clayton, co-manager of the Court Theatre with Arthur Cecil, Clayton expressed doubts about a play which showed a mother and a daughter in love with the same man.[4]

Act One begins satirically with topical reference to the women's rights movement, which attracts, Pinero implies, women frustrated in love and causes some of them to frustrate their own daughters. Mrs. Boyle-Chewton, a plainly dressed, domineering woman who is oblivious of her daughter's lack of a normal girlhood, receives the greatest share of gentle fun. Lady Vivash, her aristocratic colleague, admits with commendable self-knowledge that her interest in the movement gives her an "intoxication, an oblivion": she is haunted by memories of having rejected her lover, Philip Lyster, years before to marry out of spite the late Lord Vivash. On learning of her daugher Sylvia's unexpected return from the Continent, she exhibits a maternal excitement that makes her ridiculous as a leader of mannish women agitators. And, within minutes, she receives other exciting news: that Sylvia has fallen in love with an American poet, Ira Lee, who fortunately does not whittle or do other quaint things expected of Americans; that Lee will appear at a party on the following Wednesday to be appraised as her future son-in-law; and that Philip Lyster will "come to life" again at the same party. On hearing this, Lady Vivash, whose name is an oxymoron suggesting "live ash(es)," rushes to her dressmaker's in order to resurrect her old self as nearly as possible. The ending of the first act creates expectations of happy endings to these aristocrats' love stories, and it has turned away from satire.

Act Two begins with genial satire of the hosts and guests at a London "evening entertainment." In the farcical subplot, young

Rhoda Boyle-Chewton, jealous of Sylvia's lover, accepts the proposal of Mr. Bargus, who resembles a middle-aged cupid, curls
and all, and who has espoused the women's cause in Parliament.
But, when Bargus asks Mrs. Boyle-Chewton's permission, she
misunderstands his vague oratory as a proposal to herself and
accepts. In the main plot, a more romantic parallel occurs. A much-
changed Lady Vivash enters late, looking as young as many con-
ferences with her dressmaker could make her look, and is recognized by Ira Lee (actually Philip Lyster) not by her appearance
but by means of a token, a bracelet which he had given her. They
indulge in mutual recriminations for their "unmanly" and "un-
womanly" behavior in their lovers' quarrel years before, both implying regret for lost happiness. When Sylvia joins them with the
ironic remark that she is glad to see that they already know each
other, Lady Vivash faints; for only then does she realize that she
and her daughter love the same man.

Both tangled romances must be arranged in the final act. Even
with the aid of Mrs. Boyle-Chewton's sophisticated brother, Dudley Silchester, Bargus fails to avoid embarrassment in clearing
up her misunderstanding. Disillusioned, she laments how weak
women are; and Bargus bows out of their lives. The other problem is resolved less satisfactorily. Lady Vivash subdues her romantic feelings and, acting on maternal motives, offers to go away
if Lee-Lyster will take Sylvia and be happy. In the original ending, used in the provincial tryout production, Lee does marry Sylvia; but, for the London performances in 1889 [5] and in the printed
text, the author strengthened the parallelism in the two plots by
letting both end in renunciation: Lee-Lyster slips away, leaving
both women unfulfilled, just as Bargus has in the farcical under-
plot. Dudley Silchester, though in love with Lady Vivash, also
remains unmatched at the final curtain.

Pinero used the women's rights movement not as the subject of
the play, as commentators have assumed who have chided him for
shallowness in treating it, but topically. Only Act One, titled
"Rights and Wrongs," deals with it very specifically. Tone in each
of the acts shifts from satire to sentiment. Generally, the characters' ridiculous behavior results from touching attempts to com-
pensate for love's disappointments. Pinero could not satirize the
sincere sentiments of disappointed lovers (to him their condition
was too serious); thus he satirized the behavior of two thwarted

women who try in an unusual way to make a new life for themselves and for other women, implying that women's proper business is to be loving creatures and good mothers; when they assume other duties, they are comical.

Even more than *Imprudence,* this play is plotted to illustrate a theme: that most lives are a blend of ridiculous behavior and pathetic behavior, both arising from frustration in love. Bargus in one speech expresses a settled view on the near impossibility of happiness in love and of romantic love in marriage:

Love reminds me of the goose at one of our little county dinners. There it is at the head of the table, rich and tempting, all eyes upon it and all mouths watering. Every plate is sent up, and the carver, like Cupid, rises to the occasion—and what is the result? Only two out of a dozen get a good cut, and before an hour is over those two are extremely sorry for it. But . . . two persons walking soberly through life under one umbrella, cheerfully accepting the drippings of Providence down the backs of their necks—that's an elevating spectacle. (p. 86)

The metaphorical linking of frustration and gastronomical disappointment echoes what must have been Pinero's view since it occurs in many plays. Because Bargus is a cupid figure, the speech is ironic, though in character for him as a politician. In the diction of the other characters Pinero attained a firm evenness, sophistication, even an occasional brightness, as in Lee-Lyster's soliloquy when he is waiting to be approved as Sylvia's fiancé: "If they don't inspect me quickly I shall be an octogenarian." The language at least approximates the polish required for a comedy of manners, and the blending of satire and sentiment shows what would become characteristic of Pinero's style as a chronicler of manners. He shows upper-class characters expressing sincere feelings of love and even performing heroic acts of renunciation—not as concerned primarily with *mots* and manners—and thus illustrates his diagnosis of the sentimentality of his age.

II Mayfair

In 1884–85 Pinero found time to adapt Victorien Sardou's "well-made" play, *Maison Neuve,* to English settings and manners as *Mayfair,* a five-act comic drama. Because his French was not especially good, he worked from a literal translation and tried "to give an English play in place of a French one, and where I smell a foreign joke to find a good British substitute, if not equivalent." [6]

In its superficiality and contrivance, *Mayfair* deserves Shaw's epithet, "Sardoodledum." It relies on a visit from an old school chum for exposition, uses coincidences, and has some highly contrived but exciting scenes (notably one bedroom scene in which the seeming corpse of the heroine's potential seducer must be assumed to be hidden from her husband's view, though he remains in plain view of the audience). It is the most "well-made" of Pinero's early plays.

Once the uncomfortably stuffy life which young Agnes Roydant and her stock broker husband Geoffrey endure in his uncle's house in Bloomsbury has been revealed, the play veers off into a moralizing version of their fashionable new life in Mayfair in a home of their own. There they give parties and attract various charming but parasitic friends to their circle. Geoffrey has an affair with another woman, gambles, embezzles, and eventually ruins himself financially. Agnes nearly compromises herself with Lord Sulgrave, their house guest; and she has an even narrower scrape when she nearly kills him (or so she thinks) with a draught of a sleeping potion. In the end, Agnes and Geoffrey salvage their finances and their marriage by returning to the simple old life in Bloomsbury, where Uncle Nicholas genially puts ready cash at Geoffrey's disposal, a move which seems out of keeping with Uncle Nicholas's earlier, unfavorable portrayal.

Pinero drew the romantic entanglements explicitly for thrills, and he struck a new note in his increased attention to the psychology of the heroine. Agnes is motivated to two impulsive and crucial decisions by jealousy or a sense of being neglected: in Act Two, she reverses her decision to send Lord Sulgrave away and instead, when Geoffrey slights her on their anniversary, asks Sulgrave to have lunch alone with her; in Act Three, when she discovers Geoffrey's philandering, she writes passionately to Sulgrave inviting him to her bedroom so that she may have revenge on her wayward husband. The major blemish of the play is its lack of consistency in approach and theme, so that it appears to be only a framework for the climactic moments in it. The moralizing tone, adapted from Sardou, prevents the play from being a true comedy of manners. Though *Mayfair* affords a glimpse of the lives of the

élite in the most fashionable section of London, it contains much
potentially serious matter and finally descends to the tone of a
mystery thriller. Ironically, the author who is sometimes considered the chief English imitator of Sardou and Eugene Scribe
worked uneasily in the straitjacketing form of the "well-made"
play.

III   The Hobby Horse

In *The Hobby Horse* (1886), Pinero included considerable potentially sentimental material but carefully checked the tendency
to sentimentalize; and the result is a genuine comedy. Its satire of
sentimental philanthropists may have arisen from a current fashionable craze for "slumming" alluded to in the pages of *Punch* for
1886,[7] the same vogue which may have inspired Shaw to begin
Widowers' Houses. In *The Hobby Horse*, comic marital discord
arises from the divergent philanthropic interests of the Spencer
Jermyns. Spencer, whose comic flaw is his excessive fondness for
horse racing coupled with a misguided concern for turf folk, in-
tends to convert some of his property into a home for retired jockeys; Diana, his second wife, secretly hopes to put the same property to use as a foundlings' home, since she has no children of her
own. If there are mythological overtones in her name, they are
appropriate to her desire to protect tender young things. Both
Diana and Spencer ride their hobbyhorses so hard that they, like
the reformers in *The Weaker Sex*, seem to lack genuine concern
for each other. The main plot leads to a removal of these comic
flaws.

The minor plot contributes handily to the theme of deficient
love and also to the catharsis of laughter and ridicule. It centers
on Jermyn's son, Allan, who ran away from home to join the navy
after a quarrel with his father. Jermyn, now ready to apologize,
has employed his solicitor to locate the sailor. In Act Two, called
"A Chapter of Sentiment," Allan, disguised only by an assumed
name, turns up as a boarder at the East-End lodgings of the
clergyman Noel Brice, an advocate of the social gospel and the
most liberal and appealing of Pinero's clerical folk. Allan has
fallen in love with Bertha, Brice's niece, and comically expects a
prodigal son's reception when he takes her home as the new
daughter-in-law. Brice has fallen in love with a woman who has
been hired to relieve him of his charitable duties so that he can go

on vacation. She is actually Diana, who is taking the place of another woman who had suddenly withdrawn from practical philanthropy at the call of love. After visiting the poverty-stricken inhabitants of one particularly drab slum area, she decides that they "ought to be visited and consoled by machinery." The shrewish rector's wife comes in person to dismiss Brice for the scandal that is growing up about him and Diana because "in dealing a blow the sympathetic cadences of the human voice are much preferable" to letters. Now that Diana must leave, Brice manages to propose to her, still thinking that she is a single woman. At this instant, Jermyn and his solicitor enter searching for Allan; and Jermyn overhears the proposal.

In the final act, the two plots coalesce too neatly. By coincidence, Brice has answered Jermyn's advertisement for a superintendent for his jockey farm. The clear-eyed cleric immediately perceives that the inmates are taking advantage of Jermyn's good nature to rob him; and he exposes them, thereby disillusioning Jermyn and curing him of his misguided philanthropy. When the jockeys are ejected, Allan and Bertha as newlyweds can easily be accommodated in the house. The problem of the minister in love with a married woman, a more challenging one to solve, is also handled in a truly comic fashion. Pinero did not this time allow an inconvenient character in a triangle to succumb to the well-known "malady of the last act" in order to make way for a happy union of the remaining two, as he had done in *The Squire*. Instead, Brice manfully resigns himself to disappointment; and a speech of Jermyn's puts just the right comical finish on the situation: "Mr. Brice, Mrs. Jermyn tells me I am to beg your pardon. I do so. I have married a very foolish headstrong lady—I beg your pardon. Mrs. Jermyn keeps your niece company and assists you in your parish work without my permission—I beg your pardon. In the meantime you fall in love with my wife, sir, and you ultimately propose marriage to her in my presence—I beg your pardon." The denouement makes it clear that Spencer Jermyn will be seen less frequently at the racetrack and that Diana will more often be seen with him there—and both will help Noel Brice to find another position.

It seems wholly inaccurate to call *The Hobby Horse* a sneering comedy and to aver that Pinero in it showed his contempt of philanthropy, as Nicoll does.[8] Pinero makes no sweeping condemnation of the practice of philanthropy; he merely satirizes the special behavior of some unusually idealistic philanthropists. He once again suggests that people turn to altruistic behavior because of frustration in their domestic lives. Jermyn's foolish scheme backfires because he is muddle-headedly idealistic, having demanded that twenty honest, sober retired jockeys be found to inhabit the farm. Unfortunately, there is no necessary plot connection between his regret over alienating his son and his scheme for philanthropy. Diana, who is drawn more sympathetically than her husband and whose problem is more serious, finds that she cannot console, nurse, and love children who are not her own; and her worthwhile project suffers when confrontation with its ugly reality staggers her. Furthermore, Brice, feeling mental pain and disillusionment after his dismissal, is moved at that moment to propose to Diana, taking an immediate good, love of her, as a substitute for his more abstract satisfaction in his work. The play poses a question about what true philanthropy is, and it ends by indicating that it is at least not the behavior of egocentric idealists bent on ministering indiscriminately to some class or group, while neglecting those within the family circle.

The presence of some unsavory turf characters makes this play somewhat atypical for a manners comedy, but *The Hobby Horse* more artistically than earlier plays blends low with high characters and farcical with potentially serious matter. In the theater of its day, it was not successful, perhaps because these mixtures made audiences uneasy about what response they were to make, and because the questionable taste of the minister's romance disturbed them.

IV The Times

The Times (1891) also is slightly atypical of the comedy of manners in that it too does not deal exclusively with fashionable and would-be fashionable characters; but its intention, as stated by Pinero in an introductory note, was to touch "with a hand not too heavy some of the surface faults and follies of the hour." Defensively, perhaps, after *The Profligate* (see Chapter 6), he assured the reader that this comedy laid bare no horrid social wound, dealt with no vital and perplexing problem. If the play dealt with any question, it was whether the depths "of ignorance, of vulgarity of mind, of vanity, and of self-seeking" could be sounded. He hoped that there were some theatergoers "to whom the spectacle of the mimic castigation of the lighter faults of humanity [might] prove entertaining."

The Times has a plot which leads to the unmasking of all its hypocritical characters. Again Pinero used the three-track formula for plotting, centering the major plot on Percy Egerton-Bompas, a tradesman who has risen to wealth and membership in the House of Commons, and his wife and letting a lesser story involve each of their children. In one minor plot their daughter, Beryl, recognizes their coarseness and apologizes for them to her suitor, Denham, Viscount Lurgashall, with whom she shares disenchantment with society and all its shams. Though this earnest girl decides in the middle of the play that she is too common for her aristocratic lover and breaks off their engagement, Denham just as earnestly determines to have her, overlooking her father's buffoonery. In the other minor plot, Howard Bompas, an Oxford student, sets up a series of farcical complications by unexpectedly marrying and bringing his coarse Irish bride and his mother-in-law home in Act One. Most important of the results is the parents' attempt, with the aid of a "puffer" or publicity agent, to conceal Howard's marriage and yet make the best of it by putting the two Irish women through rigorous training to make them fit for London society. Meanwhile, the women must pose as missionaries returned from the Dakota Indians! When they are sufficiently polished, Howard can announce an engagement and all will be well.

But the impulsive nature of women has its way, and the mother-in-law leaves to have a romance of her own with a member of Parliament who is Bompas's enemy; her disclosure of the entire truth to him leads to Bompas's political downfall. In suddenly announcing his decision to resign his seat, retire from business, and live abroad, this bourgeois gentleman offers a far too assertive and self-aware explanation:

It is "getting on in the world" that has ruined me. . . . A self-taught man must always be a proud fool; he has a double share of vanity—the vanity of the ready pupil and the vanity of the successful tutor combined! He is blown out till he bursts! I say there ought to be a law to stop men like me from "getting on" beyond a certain point. Prosperity weakens our brains and hardens our hearts; it takes honest friends from us and seats things like that [Trimble, his puffer-parasite] in their chairs; it spoils good wives and breeds bad children. (p. 190)

Adequate motivation cannot be found for ths abrupt reversal in character, which is expected largely to bear the weight of the entire denouement. The satire, consistent almost to the final scene, castigates the vulgar, risen middle-class tradesman; his wife, who urges him at one point to drop an old friend as no longer advantageous to them; their almost stupid son studying at Oxford; a disreputable lady journalist, who passes off her illegitimate daughter as her niece and who prostitutes her journal for personal revenge; and the society which will presumably admit even two such outlandish persons as the Irish women, if they speak and behave properly. But Pinero especially vents his contempt on Montague Trimble, the publicity agent and confidential secretary in Bompas's employ. Trimble, whose name is significant, is the most original character in the play; and Fyfe, writing in 1902, testified that a number of such men were evident in London society at that time. He especially pointed to Trimble's "insinuating manner, his anxiety to please, his habit of sucking lozenges, his low cunning when difficulties have to be met, his selfish annoyance when his ingenuity fails to avert unpleasant occurrences" as making him a "creation, a valuable footnote to the social history of the period." [9]

Despite the somewhat unconvincing resolution, many good touches are found in the play. Surprisingly, the diction, especially in the exchanges between Beryl and Denham, approaches the style of Oscar Wilde, whose first success was yet to appear. They speak thus in Act One:

BERYL: What a wearisome affair is a Season, isn't it?
DENHAM: A Season?
BERYL: I don't mean either of the four seasons sent by Heaven; I mean the fifth, made by Man.
DENHAM: The one Season honoured by a capital letter.
BERYL: And called *the* Season. Ugh!
DENHAM: I know you care very little for gaiety.
BERYL: The gaiety of climbing a flight of stairs to clutch at a haggard hostess on the landing! (p. 6)

Fyfe commends *The Times* for truly bringing out the pathos of the "new man's" position in society; thus, to him, it is a play of sentiment.[10] Nicoll considers that Pinero is only satirically tilting against social aspiration in the play, and he faults him for a

method which is "spiritually lacking in power and in sympathy."
The social climber may be treated, he says, either farcically or
seriously, from society's or the individual's point of view; but
Pinero is content to sneer right down to the sentimental ending.[11]
Pinero in his preface called *The Times* a comedy which may "lean
more to the side of satire than sentiment." If one cannot find a
unity of tone in the play, one can discern a unity of theme. And all
the plots reveal this theme: that the code of society, if followed,
forces one to deceive or pretend, that the code can be broken with
impunity, and that hypocrisy must be exposed. All the secrets are
exposed in the various plots, and all exposures have fairly mild
consequences. The unmasking of Egerton-Bompas is accompanied by his determination to live henceforward to please himself,
not others. Howard's misalliance and Denham's show the individual acting on his inner desires, each taking his mate on her own
personal worth rather than at society's value; they disregard
labels. The characters are ridiculous as long as they try to avoid
this sane behavior. When they act according to their sentiments,
they are not objects of satire.

Aside from the interest of the play in connection with Pinero's
development as a playwright, *The Times* has some significance as
the first English play to be published after the United States
passed a statute giving protection to works published in this
country by foreign authors.[12] It was the first of a series of
twenty-one of Pinero's plays published by William Heinemann,
and it was also the first text to be distributed as an accompani-
ment to a play's production since Robert Browning's *A Blot in
the 'Scutcheon* in 1843.[13] In one of his few prefaces—in fact,
one of his few critical utterances—Pinero stated that he had
long wanted to give critics and audiences a complete text in this
way. He thought that the procedure would dignify the calling of
the actor and the craft of the playwright, allowing spectators to
give to each a fair share of credit or blame. This desire actually
amounts to a somewhat jealous concern for appropriate recognition of the stage directions as *his* contribution to the total performance. Though Pinero had been an actor himself, he does not
here seem to have been concerned for the actor's "credit or
blame"; instead, he seems to have been trying to elevate the playwright's prestige.

V   The Benefit of the Doubt

After 1891, Pinero put aside for a time the formula for comedy of manners, though he used certain sophisticated men-of-the-world characters in two tragic plays, *The Second Mrs. Tanqueray* (1893) and *The Notorious Mrs. Ebbsmith* (1895 [see Chapter 6]). When he returned to sophisticated comedy, he produced a masterwork, *The Benefit of the Doubt* (1895), written quickly when public interest in *The Notorious Mrs. Ebbsmith* began to wane.[14] Though *The Benefit of the Doubt* has usually been considered a serious play, it yields quite readily to analysis as a comedy of manners; and it would afford great pleasure if acted as such. The action concerns a woman, Theophila Fraser, who, though not guilty of any immorality, has violated the code of propriety by entertaining a married "chum," John Allingham, late at night when her husband was away. As a consequence, John's morbidly jealous wife, Olive, has brought suit for a judicial separation.

Act One takes place at the home of Theo's mother, Mrs. Emptage, where Theo's family gathers on the afternoon of the final session of the trial. As Clayton Hamilton points out, the exposition is ingenious; for the entire scene in the courtroom is revealed piecemeal—and optimistically—by successive entrances of the characters, each of whom has left the courtroom at a later moment; and the character of each one entering is revealed by what he says and by how he reacts. The effect is "to open a clear window on an all-important scene offstage." [15] A first-night reviewer said, "The sense of dramatic irony is strongly and yet delicately suggested. We foresee a 'peripety,' apparent prosperity suddenly crumbling into disaster, within the act itself; and when it comes, it awakens our sympathy and redoubles our interest." [16] Theo herself, entering last of all with her husband, must dampen all their spirits by announcing the judge's decision that she is entitled to "the benefit of the doubt," which is of course tantamount to public disgrace for her. To this catastrophe everyone reacts out of comically self-centered concern for the consequences to himself. The only way to erase the stigma, or so Theo thinks, is to do a great deal of entertaining of the "best" people in the company of her husband. But, when she learns that he insists on their going abroad for several years and that he is unable to show society that he gives her the "benefit of the doubt," she walks out, leaving her

wedding ring in a note for him. Her strong-minded aunt, Harriet
Cloys, wife of the Bishop of St. Olpherts, sets out to locate her,
divining that Theo will seek comfort in a chat with Jack Allingham at his Surrey cottage.

The second act has a clever "listening scene" which is as comically ironic as the well-known seduction scene in Molière's *Tar-
tuffe*. Pinero immediately establishes that the room in the cottage
where Allingham is entertaining bachelor friends nocturnally has
two adjoining rooms, in one of which every word spoken from the
main acting area can be heard distinctly.[17] Those who interrupt
Jack's attempt to forget his unhappiness are, first, his jealous wife,
who arrives to seek reconciliation; then Mrs. Cloys with her
brother and nephew, to look for Theo; and then Theo, to borrow
money. Mrs. Cloys and her companions, when they appear so
unceremoniously, must humorously pretend that they have come
as prospective tenants to inspect the cottage; and their dilemma
affords the pleasure of extended irony. When Olive learns that
Theo is waiting to see Jack "on a matter of business," she cannot
contain her jealousy. She insists on waiting in the next room to
overhear their conversation, promising that, if Theo's talk proves
her innocence, she will make public restitution to Theo by entertaining her as a friend. But, having arranged to signal when she
has heard enough, she comically allows the interview to continue
too long. Having had no food, Theo, under the quick influence of
a glass of champagne, blurts out her indifference to what society
will now think and invites Jack to go away to Paris with her. In a
climactic confrontation of the two women, Theo faints when she
realizes that she has been overheard.

In Act Three, Theo, "excessively weak and shattered," is recovering from her collapse. Her family gathers around her; and, for
genuine humor, Pinero exploits Jack's and Fraser's anger, their
evasion of each other, and their remorse. Theo, when given the
opportunity to explain her behavior of the night before by saying
that she was "not herself," demurs: "It *was* myself, the dregs of
myself, that came to the top last night!" Having had a deep look
inside herself and a moral awakening, she cannot accept a merely
social redemption. She rejects, therefore, both Fraser's and Olive
Allingham's sincere offers to do all possible, socially, to rehabili-
tate her reputation. Instead, she agrees to be taken under her
Aunt Harriet's wing and to live at the Bishop's palace or his town

house for a year or so. The Bishop and Mrs. Cloys thus will mantle her in an atmosphere of ecclesiastical sobriety. In a few months, it is assumed, few tongues will wag about her, except in respectful tones; and, in a year's time, Fraser will probably reinstate her as his wife in his home.

Those who sneer at the ending as a meretricious way to salvage Theophila's reputation do not consider that, as far as the whole of society is concerned, she has already been exonerated (technically) by the courtroom verdict and that her own family lacks charity to give her the benefit of the doubt. Now another institution, the Church, represented by the "mild-looking, very old" Bishop, comes to her aid. The entrance of this vague patriarch at the end of Act Three is needless except to incorporate ironic use of the time-honored *deus ex machina*. Thus playfully, Pinero developed his theme that, when a woman like Theo has so thoughtlessly scandalized society, drastic measures are necessary to avert catastrophe. Because she has done nothing morally wrong, the play can maintain a comic atmosphere despite its potentially serious overtones. The comic ending subtly conveys Pinero's distaste for the sham rescue which society could effect.

There are numerous opportunities for good comic acting in the play, even in so small a role as that of Quaife, Jack's servant. The diction has appropriateness to character, originality, wit, and economy. Evidently convinced of the essential self-centeredness of human beings, Pinero invented preoccupied characters and selected just the right words to convey Theo's uncle's pomposity, her brother Claude's pique and curiosity, Mrs. Emptage's self-dramatization, even Mrs. Cloys's maternal concern growing out of her own lack of children. Through speeches of several characters in Act Three, the playwright ingeniously creates the convincing impression of several actions going on at once in various rooms not shown onstage. The effect of the whole is to give a delightful portrait of a large, late-Victorian family.

VI   The Princess and the Butterfly

In Pinero's next comedy of manners he again treated his audience to the spectacle of aristocrats who act on the longings of the heart rather than on reason or prudence in order to gain happiness. *The Princess and the Butterfly; or, The Fantasticks* (1897), a delicate theme-centered play about middle age, invites close com-

parison with Chekhov in its quiet action, in its characters who fear
that they will spoil their own futures, and in its mixture of sympathy and ridicule in the same characters. In the play, Laura, the
Princess Pannonia, widowed after twenty years of a "sensible"
marriage to an aged prince, returns to London only to find dis-
tressing memories of her girlhood, consciousness of her wasted
years, and malaise. She finds sympathy and understanding in Sir
George Lamorant, the middle-aged brother of her long-dead
suitor. Since all that Sir George sees about him is "tombstones," he
has determined to flit about to places where he does not remember being young. When they later meet in Paris, it seems that a
sensible marriage might be their cure for middle age. But their
situation is complicated by the looming presence of a young lover
for each of them: Fay Zuliani, Sir George's ward who is full of the
joy of living and who falls in love with him; and Edward Oriel, a
presumably cold-blooded diplomat, who falls passionately in love
with the Princess and completely reverses his behavior and mode
of dressing in his role as ardent swain. For a time, the older pair
seem destined to behave in a sane and logical way; but, in a tricky
final scene, each submits to impulse and instead accepts a flutter-
ing young thing for a mate. Both gain courage to do what society
regards as a foolish thing; and they are thereby true to themselves, whether they come any nearer to true happiness or not.

By Pinero's conduct of the action and his character portrayals,
he develops the theme that, in the crucial time of middle age,
people try various methods of surviving their boredom, their consciousness of lost opportunities, and their awareness of encroach-
ing age. Most of the action of the first two acts is shaped by this
theme, and some of it is symbolic. Act One includes much talk of
middle age on the occasion of Laura's fortieth birthday. Sir
George argues that a man has as much reason as a woman to be
concerned with middle age: "The same tide rises in both—rises,
beats merrily against their ribs for a few years, and then ebbs. It's
an uncomfortable sensation . . . to hear the lapping of that tide
as it turns within you and begins to do down." Laura, on receiv-
ing a bracelet made of gilt three-penny pieces, one for each year,
determines to get accustomed to the weight of it (her years). A
friend, Mrs. St. Roche, remarks that a clever woman can avoid
having a "middle" age by prolonging the period when she is attractive to men and by hurrying the onset of the time when she

neither expects nor receives their devotion, thus cutting out the interval of wretchedness. Middle-aged herself, Mrs. St. Roche follows her own advice, as later action shows, by having affairs with younger men. Other characters offer or represent different cures: travel, gourmandizing, centering one's life in one's children, lavish entertaining of younger people.

An evening gala at the St. Roches' provides the atmosphere for the second act, which is "a brilliant sketch of social smartness" with satiric overtones.[18] Most of their guests are fools, fops, and parasites. One young guest recommends a return to the coarser, more elemental pleasures of an earlier age, and dresses in a fashion to suggest it. Another, noted for his collection of toys, demonstrates an air ball resembling a human head; when it loses air, it emits a despairing screech, wrinkles, and collapses. Its performance is an uncomfortable emblem to Sir George, who is supposed to be cheered by the festivities. When talk turns to the theater, Fay offers pertinent criticism of a play which she has just seen: she says that English actors cannot act because decorum demands that they do everything, even murder, with their respectable fingertips. Almost immediately a crisis of respectability arises: Sir George, by exposing the low reputation of one of the women at the party, angers her escort and thus provokes a duel with the young man, without Fay's knowledge.

In the remaining acts, however, the plot becomes less theme-centered. The third contrasts Edward's ardent proposal and Sir George's suggestion of a sensible match, leading to Laura's ordering each man to wait one month for an answer. The fourth performs several functions in a workmanlike way: it builds suspense before the duel, it brings Fay and Sir George together for a revelation of his intention to fight the duel, and it leads up to her climactic realization that she loves him more than a ward ordinarily would.

The restrained fifth act does not show the duel but moves forward a month to a time when Sir George has nearly completed his recovery from his wound—and from "respectability," figuratively. Here Laura makes her choice between the two men, remembering also that "respectable" people allowed her to contract her unhappy first marriage. After some rather stagy maneuvers to bring about the reversals, Pinero gives her a cue—some band music offstage playing a song which says that love is ever young; and she chooses Edward. Sir George, more ironically aware that love is also often blind, takes Fay. Laura's aunt remarks chorally that they seem like foolish dream people, fantastic creatures; but Pinero leaves another interpretation open: his careful control of tone suggests wistful sympathy with the lovers as well as their potential folly. This quiet act of "justified anticlimax" [19] would have been entirely different if Pinero had merely wanted to write a "well-made" piece with many thrilling complications and a neat resolution of the ending. George Alexander, who produced the play at his theater, wrote, "The last act, too, is startling in its genius, with its manipulation of 'the fairy tale, happy for ever after' ending—it fairly takes one's breath away, it is so delicate, so profound and so limitlessly human in its analysis." [20] Thus he paid tribute to Pinero's skill in achieving the right balance between sentiment and irony.

Perhaps audiences and critics chose to interpret the ending as a straight happy-forever-after one, since the play had popular but not critical success. In accounting for its relative failure, Fyfe pointed out that "it defied tradition, it outraged the accepted canons of form and symmetry [in having five acts instead of three, usual for comedy], its originality even hurled itself against the salutary barriers of common sense." [21] But W. L. Courtney early recognized the mastery inherent in the piece: he thought its "easy garrulity . . . never meaningless" but "ever and anon lit up with flashes of polished wit . . . clever . . . but always 'dramatic'." Pointing out that "it is of the essence of the comic idea to find that all prudential maxims, wise saws, and modern instances fail helplessly in the attempt to guard the human heart against folly," he suggested that Pinero had broadened the art of comedy by writing this play. [22] Nicoll called it "a truly excellent sentimentalized comedy of manners" which shows Pinero's genuine gift for comedy. Its characters' "artificiality and the contrast between that artificiality and natural impulse provide Pinero with material of which he makes good use. Nearly does he succeed in his attempt to enter that dream world which Charles Lamb saw in the comedy of Congreve." [23] On the whole, the play has sound craftsmanship, subtlety of tone, dazzling scenes of social gaiety, and a relevant sociological outlook (in its treatment of middle age) that recommend it for revival.

VII The Gay Lord Quex

By the time that Pinero achieved his highest mark in writing social comedy, he had before him the example of Wilde's plays and Henry Arthur Jones's *The Case of Rebellious Susan* (1894) and *The Liars* (1897). He may have aspired to equal or to surpass these achievements, or, responding to the favorable criticisms which had called *The Second Mrs. Tanqueray* the best English play since Sheridan's *The School for Scandal*, to equal the style of Sheridan. Though he could not consciously have been composing a valedictory to the Victorian era, the play *The Gay Lord Quex* (1899), seems most un-Victorian; for it harks back to Restoration and eighteenth-century comedy of manners and looks forward to Pinero's series of plays which reflect the much freer Edwardian manners. That this play was the only one of his to be published on fine paper with hard covers in a limited edition is indicative of the opinion that it would last.

Like many comedies of manners, *The Gay Lord Quex* uses certain stock characters, notably two rakes: the Marquess of Quex, who in middle age has reformed and is ready to settle into a respectable marriage; and, by contrast, his unregenerate companion in debauchery on many former occasions, Sir Chichester Frayne. The Duchess of Strood is a slightly wicked middle-aged siren who threatens Quex's success. The young, demure, "typically English creamy girl" about to be forced into marriage with the worldly Quex is Muriel Eden. But there is a prominent character who is something of an anomaly, Sophy Fullgarney, foster-sister to Muriel, who, having begun as maid in various upper-class families, has risen to the proprietorship of a manicurist's parlor. Coming as she does from the lower classes, she acts on presumably genuine sentiments of revulsion at the knowledge of Quex's past and tries to prevent the marriage. But, in doing so, she grossly breaches upper-class etiquette and creates what turns out to be much ado over nothing.

Act One contains interesting local color, taking place in Sophy's Bond Street place of business, where members of two worlds, the fashionable aristocrats and the manicurists, mingle and where Muriel, unchaperoned, can plausibly meet the young man whom she thinks she loves, Captain Napier Bastling. But the main business of the first two acts is to make plausible Sophy's presence for

a night at Fauncey Court, a grand country house, and to set the
stage for the big scene of Act Three, a battle of wits between
Sophy and the gay Lord Quex, whose wickedness she is determined to expose.

Failing at flirting with him, Sophy contrives to take the place of
the Duchess of Strood's maid in order to eavesdrop on the Duchess, whom she has overheard insisting on a rendezvous with the
reluctant Quex late at night. When Sophy is discovered at the key-
hole, Quex sends the Duchess away in order to save her reputation and locks himself in with Sophy, hoping to bargain with her
for silence. Reconciled to being discovered with Sophy the next
morning and to the loss of Muriel, he threatens to ruin Sophy's
reputation and her chance of happiness with her fiancé. She now
must concede him the upper hand, writing a letter which puts
herself in his power. But, in another thrilling reversal, she realizes
that she cannot thus hand Muriel over to him and pulls the servants' bell to denounce him. Her self-sacrificial dedication to Muriel's happiness so impresses him that he now saves Sophy by
helping her to dismiss the summoned servants. Grateful and convinced that he is not completely wicked, she promises "to do what
she can" for him. Of this exciting climax, F. S. Boas, writing in
1936, has testified, "Across all the years that have flown since 1899
I can still hear that duel of wits on the stage of the Globe Theatre,
and can still see Miss Vanbrugh [the actress] tugging at that bell-
rope." [24]

Sophy keeps her promise in Act Four. The next day, back at her
manicurist's parlor, she lies to Muriel, indicating that she discovered nothing to prove Quex's profligacy. Even so, Muriel, when
intending to say good-bye to Captain Bastling, impulsively promises to marry the soldier. When Quex learns this outcome of their
secret meetings, he thinks that Sophy has betrayed him. Now the
dramatist must reach deep into his bag of tricks to effect a satis-
factory ending. He succeeds by allowing Sophy to repeat her trick
of deceptive flirting, this time on Bastling, who, ironically, proves
a would-be philanderer. When Muriel sees them kissing, she accepts the disillusionment and agrees to be a good wife to Quex.
The happiness of the two strongly conflicting characters, the
slightly vulgar manicurist and the witty marquess, is thus assured.

All of the twists and turns in this obviously "well-made" plot
take place within a supposed twenty-four hours. Since the *scène à*

faire in the third act seems to be its reason for existence, the play can be adequately described as a play about a bedroom, with two acts of prologue and one of epilogue. Indeed, criticism of the play has centered on the bedroom scene. Fyfe called it the most ingenious scene that Pinero ever wrote and the cleverest since Sheridan's screen scene. But the play does not, as he thought, merely show how "exceedingly unpleasant people of rank and fashion" can be, with the "manners of organ-grinders and the morals of monkeys," or appeal entirely to the head, as a picture of the low moral tone of the age.[25] Instead, for a mixed audience containing both aristocrats (of blood, intellect, or talent) and members of the middle class, it objectively "contrasts the manners of the aristocracy with the manners of the lower classes and sets forth a tense and thrilling struggle between the different ideals" of Quex and Sophy.[26] In some measure, "amoral" correctly describes the tone of the action. Both Sophy and Muriel turn out to be making too much of a fuss; sensible women simply adopt the way of the world and accept men for what they *all* are. On the other hand, Quex's reformation seems to be curiously genuine.

VIII Letty

Another play which balances sophisticated manners and middle-class scrupulosity is *Letty* (1903). Though it seems considerably like a problem play about marriage between classes and somewhat like a sentimental comedy, it is a comedy of manners which with subtle irony demonstrates the gradual disillusionment of its heroine, leading to a healthy, realistic adjustment of her life in an epilogue.

The orphaned heroine, Letty, has a middle-class background and works among lower middle-class surroundings, but she dreams of ideal happiness (marriage, wealth, sophisticated living) with Neville Letchmere, a gentleman whose name cannot be ignored. The irony of her dream is revealed when the audience learns (before she does) that Letchmere is married but separated from his wife. When she learns that she can not expect to marry him, she abridges her notion of happiness and accepts the proposal of her employer, a Jew named Mandeville ("man of the City"), who will give her wealth; and, because an illness prevents her from working any longer, she must choose a provider. Though she tries to overlook his gaucherie, she realizes at a celebration of her

engagement that she could not bear life with him. Her abandoning the party at the end of Act Three to visit Letchmere late at
night leads predictably to a crisis concerning her reputation in Act
Four. Just as she seems determined to give up her scruples and
settle for comfort and gaiety without the benefit of marriage,
chance intervenes to save her. A note arrives from Letchmere's
married sister, whom he had been trying to confirm in her good
intentions of saying good-bye to a paramour until Letty's plight
distracted him. Though he had hoped that she would become the
first Letchmere to avoid scandal and unhappiness, she has run
away with her lover. His remorse is apparent to Letty, who, sens-
ing for the first time the impossibility of happiness with Letchmere, leaves. Her departure results from no heroic act of the will
but only from a crucial and final disillusionment occasioned by
chance. Having tried and rejected both means to a new life within
twelve hours, she now seemingly faces an impasse.

The play proper ends here, with a climactic moment which
would ordinarily be placed at the end of the penultimate act in a
"well-made" play. It does not prepare for the Epilogue, which
shows that Letty has taken a hidden alternative, marriage to the
unassuming photographer of the second act, and that, two and a
half years later, she is well and happy helping him in his studio.
By coincidence, an almost disabled Letchmere and his unhappy
sister come into the studio to be photographed. This action does
little more than juxtapose the robust woman and the sick man,
both contrasts to their former selves, eliciting pathos for Letchmere and acquiescence in Letty's choice of a man of her own
class.

Regrettably, this termination of the story seems like a sop to
middle-class audiences by upholding their ideals of hard work
and clean living as productive of happiness and by denigrating
the dissolute behavior of the idle rich. But it can also be said to
balance objectively the sober notion that Letty's happiness was a
consequence of her disillusionment against the sympathetic portrait of the man of means and manners. This view of Letchmere
accords not only with Pinero's pictures of aristocrats in very early
plays (see Chapter 6) but also with his almost Naturalistic emphasis on the role of heredity and environment in both central
characters' lives. To him, this ending was a happy one in the sense
that it grew out of their characters. Because of her background,

Letty would not have been happy with the aimless man, just as he could not suddenly reform his character.

In addition to drawing character convincingly, Pinero also effectively concealed his contrivances in *Letty*. The exposition of the complicated architecture of Letchmere's flat comes unnoticed while the first seventeen words are being spoken. Other information is skillfully planted to prepare for important action, such as the excessive heat in the flat which leads to Letty's fainting; the lateness of the hour in Act Three, establishing the probability of the restaurant's closing before Mandeville's elaborate order can be filled; and the rain shower which occasions Letty's need to dry her shoes and let her hair down in Act Four.[27] The chance occurrences necessary to plot and theme would seem plausible in the theater, especially since all of them are ordinary events. Mandeville's coincidentally taking his party to the restaurant where Letchmere is supping with his companions is accounted for by the likelihood of his choosing a fashionable establishment to impress Letty and her friends.

Especially noteworthy is the carefully contrived dialogue, which achieves naturalness at the same time that it maintains interest through rhythm and repetition. The best example accompanies Letty's discovery that Letchmere is a married man: she echoes her astonishment with a series of nearly similar lines, all emphasizing that the realization can only gradually sink into her consciousness. She says, "You might have mentioned it [his being married] before. You might have mentioned it." A few lines later she laments, "You—you might have mentioned her"; and still later, with greater anguish, "Oh, why didn't you mention it?" Hamilton had high praise for the "tragic repetition" of this passage.[28]

Even the choice and arrangement of settings deserve praise. The second act contains one of Pinero's most Realistic and at the same time picturesque scenes, the roof of a boarding house with a prospect of London "seen in the golden light of late afternoon" as a background. It is so "absolutely novel" and so "emphatically picturesque," according to Hamilton, that it might inspire a photographer.[29] The presence of the photographer in the cast and in the scene gives the author a chance to reuse a favorite play-within-the-play, or picture-within-a-picture, device. The scene shows art imitating life, as Pinero's play has successfully done.

IX   The "Mind the Paint" Girl

Pinero reworked old material in *The "Mind the Paint" Girl*
(1912), telling the story of an actress caught in the well-worn love
triangle against a background of theatrical life. As in *Trelawney
of the "Wells,"* the action reflects both theatrical and social history
of an era; but, lacking the charm of the earlier play, this unpopu-
lar piece was accused of libeling the contemporary stage.[30]

The title character, Lily Parradell, has earned fame by her ren-
dition of a musical comedy song, "Mind the Paint." In British
slang of the era, "minding the paint" meant leading men on without actually compromising one's reputation. Though the other
girls at the Pandora Theatre do form numerous casual attach-
ments to rich men, Lily is not a coquette. Her portrayal as a
woman not tainted by the world around her won commendation
from Hamilton, who thought that it alone justified composition of
this "comedy of atmosphere." [31] Loveless herself, she undergoes
the usual struggle of putting off the two men who offer her marriage: the jealously possessive Nicko Jeyes, who has nearly ruined
his military career through dancing attendance on her; and the
shy Lord Farncombe, who has just discovered his love for her.
The *raisonneur* Lionel Roper and Lily's other friends opt for the
aristocrat and maneuver to keep Jeyes away from her birthday
party, for they hope that Farncombe will have the chance to win
her. At the end of Act One, the story veers off into a somewhat
pointless intrigue in which Jeyes, by disguising his voice over the
telephone, discovers the arrangements and attends the party in
the guise of a waiter. The two party scenes (Act Two), which
take place in the refreshment lobby of the Pandora Theatre, are
highly undramatic and almost gratuitous, except as atmosphere.
The first consists mostly of introductions among the guests; the
second choreographically focuses on successive pairs of characters.
In each pair is a showgirl who is "minding the paint" and hinting
for lavish gifts from her escort.

Act Three, the only one designed to be dramatic, according to
Hamilton,[32] has several poorly motivated reversals, which seem to
show the playwright toying with his audience. First, Lily, entertaining Lord Farncombe in her boudoir after the party, declines
his proposal; and she recounts in one excellent speech why her
background would make her unsuitable to be his wife. Next Jeyes

appeals to her pity for his broken condition and begs her again to
go to Rhodesia with him. When he hears of Farncombe's proposal, he relinquishes her to him, as he thinks. But she now reveals
that she has rejected Farncombe; and, picturing herself as Jeyes's
savior, she vows to accept him and lift him out of his degradation.

In Act Four, another implausible reversal takes place. Jeyes,
having unaccountably become Farncombe's fast friend by the
next morning, again hands Lily over to him and bows out of her
life. Now that Lily is convinced of her love for the aristocrat and a
wedding is assured, Lily's mother comments too patently that the
match will improve Lily's manners and status as well as the vigor
of the Farncombe line.

This work evinces some interest in dialect for characterization
of several minor characters (but Shaw's *Pygmalion* in the same
year handled it more interestingly and functionally) and borders
on being a musical comedy in its frequent reprises of bits of the
title song. Undoubtedly, the play reflects the freedom of Edwardian manners and an actual tendency, begun twenty years earlier,
for members of the acting profession to attain high positions in
society. In the 1890s actresses married noblemen with growing
frequency and little scandal, and actor-managers like Squire Bancroft and Henry Irving rose to knighthoods. Similarly, younger
sons and the daughters of the upper classes became actors when
the theater attained its new respectability. But that Pinero in the
last year of his life should have called the play his best[33] is incredi-
ble.

X The Big Drum

The Big Drum (1915) has a hero who is an aristocrat only by
talent and a heroine who attains rare self-knowledge. It satirically
attacks the publicity-seeking and vulgar manners of some titled
Englishmen and reflects Pinero's dislike of publicity. For once, the
woman's choice of a mate moves somewhat into the background.

The name of the novelist-hero, Philip Mackworth, indicates his
passion for establishing his own worth by genuine industry and
talent. Detesting those who wish to be in the public eye merely
by "beating their own drums," he plans to attack them in a new
book, significantly called *The Big Drum*, which he hopes will
establish his fame honestly. In conversation before a luncheon

party at the opening of the play, his urbane friend Robert Roope as *raisonneur* counsels moderation and suggests that Philip adjust to the tendencies of the age. Roope is giving the luncheon to effect a reunion of the hero and an old friend, Ottoline, the widowed Comtesse de Chaumier. Learning of his intention, Philip says: "If Ottoline married me, she'd be puffing my wares on the sly before the honeymoon was half over!" Though most of the other guests seek the help of a journalist among them to get themselves or their pet projects known, Ottoline does not; and Philip seems to have misjudged her. After lunch, she explains to Philip that her loveless marriage, contracted to spite him, has matured her and has made her long to be free from sham and pettiness. He suggests that, when he is genuinely successful, they might return as man and wife to Paris, where they were once happy together.

Act Two grossly caricatures Ottoline's parents, Sir Randle and Lady Filson, and her brother, Bertram, as glory-seeking social climbers, though titled. Sir Randle habitually attends funerals of notables so that his name will appear in the lists of mourners. Disappointed in Ottoline's rejection of a rich baronet because the pompous announcement of the engagement was already written, they immediately recommence matchmaking. They decry her choice of a mere author until Philip explains that he does not want to marry before he is famous. On hearing the idea for his new book, they are comforted by their sneering confidence that such a book will never sell.

Several months later in Act Three, Philip is giving a dinner party to celebrate the almost phenomenal sales of his book and his engagement to Ottoline. The Filsons, who have now taken literature under their wings, are publicizing their prospective son-in-law. Philip seems pleased to have got into the papers by genuine means, but his pride collapses when a private detective employed by Ottoline's brother discloses that the books have almost all been bought by one person—Ottoline. Philip, crestfallen but thankful for the revelation of his own vanity and credulity, rebuffs Ottoline and sits down to dinner alone.

Though the play could end here, Pinero wrote a fourth act and even provided an alternate ending for it later. Philip, hoping to become reconciled with Ottoline, offers to forgive her for her vulgarity and even to give up writing to become her dependent if she wants that. With remarkable self-analysis, she explains that she is an incurably vulgar woman. One critic's objection that vulgar people never know that they are vulgar[34] is beside the point, considering that the author went to some pains to motivate the individualized heroine's change in self-knowledge. Thinking that she has already spoiled Philip's writing career, she gives him up to his art, indicating that she will accept the baronet, whom she can advertise.

Because this ending did not seem happy in 1915 to audiences preoccupied with World War I, Pinero brought about a forced reconciliation in an alternate version. But the printed text gives the original and Pinero's explanation that he did not conceive of it as in any sense unhappy: "On the contrary, I looked upon the separation of these two people as a fortunate occurrence for both; and I conceived it as a piece of ironic comedy. . . ." This bit of ironic comedy justifies the addition of the fourth act, whereas the alternate ending does not.

XI A Cold June

A Cold June (1932), written between 1929 and 1931, when Pinero was in his mid-seventies, is a very competent, brittle piece somewhat like Maugham's plays. It features a young woman whose story parallels Letty's up to a point; but this heroine, the June of the title, has no middle-class scruples. One of nature's amoral aristocrats, she cares only for luxury, ease, and charming companions. When her escape from a girls' school does not bring the happiness she longs for, she does not, like some heroines in Pinero's problem plays, commit suicide. Instead, she follows her instinctual gaiety without regard for propriety and elopes with a married man resembling Neville Letchmere; and Pinero did not feel constrained to show her as either happy or unhappy in an epilogue.

In the situation that arises from June's illegitimacy, Pinero approaches his old hilarity by providing her with three putative fathers. Two of them appear in the first scene to exhibit their concern over letters that they have received. The letters are identical; each addresses one of the middle-aged men as the father of a girl whose guardian has recently died, asking him to take care of her. Later, they endure the indignity of going before a prim schoolmistress to explain and take over their parental duties, which they will share. They have long been friends, and, in their rather liber-

tine younger days, had shared the same mistress; neither denies
the possibility that he may be the father. They expect a drab brat
of a child; but, when they meet June, they are pleasantly surprised.
Though both are now eager to protect this sophisticated charmer,
she makes her choice of them by considering their financial conditions, their addresses, and their manners. She chooses to live at the
town house of Hugo Faulkner, easily the more polished and the
wealthier of the two; but she also agrees to share some of her time
with retired Colonel Roland Twinn, a slangier, coarser man.

In succeeding action each man comes to see in June some resemblance to his own ancestors and becomes jealous of the other.
Both exhibit an annoying degree of possessiveness. When Twinn
gets temporary use of a villa on the Riviera, June agrees to go
there with him—but only if he will take her on the most luxu-
rious boats and trains; and he has to borrow money from Faulkner
in order to meet her standard. At the villa, while Faulkner is visiting there briefly, a third and much more objectionable father appears—a married man slow to accept his potential responsibility
for June. Rudely questioning him about the kind of life that
awaits her if she should agree to spend time with him, she realizes
that it will be a boring life among the "horsey" set of the provinces.

Moved to reject her duty to any of the fathers, she elopes with
the Earl of Linthrop. A well-mannered married man separated
from his wife, he has followed her from London and takes her
away on his yacht. The tables are neatly turned before Faulkner
and Twinn know it, and only at breakfast at eleven the next morning when she is far away do they discover her elopement. Since
the audience can easily understand the reason for her comic triumph over their values of respectability and their possessiveness,
it now is not expected to have any qualms about her embracing
the kind of irregular union which earlier Pineroesque heroines had
shunned. June *will* have a relationship based on inclination, not
duty.

There is excellent comedy in the peculiar way in which the men
learn of their paternity, in the rivalry that grows between them
when their expectations of their child are reversed, and in their
imagining her resemblances to their ancestors. In the dialogue the
awkwardly phrased letter is read aloud three times, with variation
in the characters' comments, to create an echo effect. Pinero

wisely delayed the entrance of the third father until the third act, where it is a surprise and affords an interesting climactic realization on the heroine's part. She suddenly acquires warmth and expresses it by bolting. This well-constructed, sophisticated play would be delightful to present-day audiences because of its amoral tone.

XII *Achievement*

The elevation of tone in English comedy that is generally recognized to have come with the plays of Wilde and Shaw is not attributable to any one man. It was prepared for by revivals of Restoration and eighteenth-century plays and by the writings of George Meredith, Robertson, Gilbert and Sullivan, Henry Arthur Jones, and Pinero. When Wilde's and Shaw's first plays appeared in 1892, they found an audience already predisposed to enjoy this genre and its effects. In creating this audience Pinero had a great share with such plays as *The Hobby Horse, The Weaker Sex,* and *The Times* as well as his sophisticated farces. Yet only Hamilton credits him with pointing forward to the style of Shaw.[35]

In his earliest comedies of manners Pinero combined the study of manners with the evocation of tender sentiment—much as Wilde's plays (excluding *The Importance of Being Earnest*) do. Later, beginning with *The Benefit of the Doubt* he adroitly balanced sophisticates against morally earnest characters in a more objective style, which *The Princess and the Butterfly* continues and *The Gay Lord Quex* crowns. Though it lacks the brilliance of Wilde and the intellectual vigor of Shaw, this latter play more nearly captures the mood and style of Sheridan than the other playwrights do. It does not materially vary the old formula except in mixing middle-class characters and manners of a more democratic age. It is gay and engaging in its own way and faithfully reflects the *beau monde* of its day. *The Big Drum* is almost Molièrean, and *A Cold June* evokes an atmosphere of Restoration nonchalance.

Though Pinero was not a great satirist, he incorporated effective satirical touches in *The Weaker Sex, The Hobby Horse,* and *The Times.* Though Hamilton detects originality in Henry Arthur Jones's satirically treating members of a large group who share the same sentiment in *The Crusaders* (1891),[36] Pinero had already done the same thing in the 1880s. Though of the middle class

himself, he had no trouble in drawing witty gentlemen. He did
not load his dialogue with artificial wit like Wilde's; with his Realistic bent he preferred to let the characters' talk avoid unnatural
brilliance. He wrote as many good plays in this genre as in the
others, yet his accomplishment as a chronicler of manners is seldom acknowledged.

CHAPTER 6

Master Architect of Problem Plays

LACKING an established genre which could serve as an adequate vehicle for serious consideration of problems, nineteenth-century playwrights had to invent a new form—the problem play. Because the type deals centrally with some social, economic, ethical, religious, marital, or sexual problem and frequently lets the denouement stand as a solution, it requires a degree of frankness and open-mindedness which was unheard of in the Victorian popular theater, where nothing was to offend the most innocent patron. As Archer early discerned, its aim is to present to audiences the most everyday events in familiar surroundings under conditions which stimulate their faculties and concentrate their attention so that they clearly apprehend "undreamt-of significance." [1]

Naturally, verisimilitude in all aspects is necessary to this end. Causes and effects must be dealt with honestly, the past considered in relation to the present, and character treated in terms of heredity and environment. When a writer adopts this scheme, he cannot be expected to produce purely tragic or purely comic results; for a drama which reproduces life faithfully must mix the comic and the serious as life does. He also must forego hackneyed situations and obviously theatrical devices of farce and melodrama. More exactly, he must obscure his contrivances by means of the art which conceals itself.

The definitive problem plays written by Continental writers were not seen in English theaters until nearly 1890, and then only in "independent" theaters, not by the broad public. Even by then, few Englishmen—men of the theater included—had heard of Henrik Ibsen. Archer's translation of *The Pillars of Society* had been given a single matinee performance in 1880, and only two or three adequate translations of Ibsen had been published.[2] A *Doll's House* had been so thoroughly adapted as *Breaking a*

Butterfly by Henry Arthur Jones and Henry Herman in 1884 as to be practically unrecognizable. When English theater patrons were later introduced to an unvarnished Ibsen play, they did not like what they saw; and a heated controversy over whether his plays should be allowed to be performed lasted till well after the passing of the Victorian era.

Evidently, no native English play before 1880 attempted to deal seriously with contemporary life as novels had been doing since the early Dickens books. Even when Dickens was adapted for the stage, adaptors generally concentrated on his genial comics and on his black-hearted villains to write comedy-melodramas in the prevailing mode; therefore, they completely neglected his social criticism. Archer, surveying English drama in 1886, saw some evidence that it might be moving toward the ideal of Ibsen: "I cannot quite lose faith in the ultimate evolution of a form of drama which shall soberly and simply reproduce the everyday aspects of modern life, without having recourse to lost wills, and mysterious murders, and Enoch-Arden bigamies, and Tweedledum-Tweedledee Twins. . . ." [3] He expressed tentative confidence that British playwrights would grope their own way to "a comedy or drama of observation."

Of those writing in the early 1880s, only three authors could have given Archer grounds for this belief. Sydney Grundy had adopted the manner of French *pièces à thèse*, but he did not succeed in motivating his characters well or in fitting them convincingly into his plots. [4] Jones had won some praise for his melodramatic *Saints and Sinners* (1884), a seduction drama dealing with scandal in a parson's family. Pinero, more than either of these, was independently seeking more plausible plotting, convincing characterization, unstereotyped language, and verisimilitude in settings. He was trying to reveal the effects of the past without putting all of the incidents onto the stage, as melodrama usually did, and without the obvious exposition of "well-made" plays. In his earliest efforts, however, he took recourse to formulas, stock farcical characters in the lower classes, and happy endings.

I   The Rector

If *The Rector: The Story of Four Friends* (1883) was a disappointment to audiences, it was nevertheless Pinero's first attempt to build a whole play about contemporary marriage problems. Its production almost coincided with his own wedding. It faintly recalls *Othello* in plot and character (Pinero had acted Roderigo at the Lyceum) but lacks a tragic resolution.

Pinero spread his action over a year's time and crowded material into each of his four acts. Yet Act One could easily have been omitted and its major incident, Humphrey Charland's falling in love at first sight, revealed in retrospect. Act Two announces the "problem," after Humphrey, the rector, and his bride, Hope, return from their honeymoon six months later. A discovery occasioned by the finding of a letter that did not reach the groom on the eve of the wedding shatters his peace of mind. Hope had written it hinting at something in her past about which she wanted never to be questioned and offering to go away if he should insist on knowing. Now Humphrey can only tear the letter up, in a magnanimous gesture, since the choice which it originally gave him is beyond recall; and a rift begins to yawn between husband and wife.

In Act Three, six months later, Humphrey and his friend Jessmond Ryle hastily conclude that Hope, known to have come from the garrison town where the third friend, Clive Morrison, committed suicide, is the woman who ruined him. Iago-like, Jessmond destroys Humphrey's last reasonable doubt by insisting that Hope is indeed the former mistress of their dead friend. But Jessmond has become so embittered about women and even neurotically jealous of Humphrey's love of Hope that he is verging on insanity. Thus delusion and jealousy supposedly explain his potential villainy. The modern Othello is by no means suspicious ("jealous") in nature, but he does have a career and happiness at stake in the purity and reputation of his wife. When he is forced to think the worst, he does not rage wildly and strangle his Desdemona; he tells her that tomorrow they must part. He longs for the Hope that used to be his; and, by the end of the play, she (it?) is restored to him through the reliable testimony of the fourth friend, a doctor who confirms Jessmond's near madness, and through Hope's confession, which reveals her father's cheating at cards, no loss of her own virtue. This accurate knowledge of the past works a happy reconciliation; and there are now four friends again—one of them a woman.

Though Pinero drew the minor characters farcically and some of them are totally extraneous, he took more care with motivation of the important characters. There is some rather modern psychological insight in the portrayal of Jessmond Ryle's obsession. One reviewer[5] objected that Pinero tricked his audience into believing that what Jessmond said of Hope was the truth, but there are enough clues to alert an audience to his delusion. Pinero showed insight into subconscious motivation when he interpreted Humphrey's overworking as being due to his marital frustration. Archer noted "a curious obliquity of moral judgment" which made the hero unsympathetic in crucial scenes;[6] but the playwright must have intended exactly this effect, rather than that of a "merely sympathetic personage." The rector is described as being forbidden by his profession "to trace the little springs which feed the great river of humanity"; that is, he has too idealistic a view of human nature. As a man of the cloth, he also cannot take an Othello-like revenge in a violent way; but he is expected to have high moral standards and a passion for honesty. Perhaps to him, his own passionate love for Hope is a failing; for he speaks of passion as being "like a young kitten—on the ninth day it opens its eyes."

This conception of the central character is an admirable one, but Pinero cheapened it by using a situation capable of having a fairy-tale ending. The problem evaporates when the rumors and imputations are discredited, and the rector's suffering seems to have been pointless. A much more genuine play could have been written around a rector who in ignorance had married a really disreputable woman. Would he resign? Would he confess to the congregation and go away? Would he reform the woman, forgiving her for her past? Or would he urge a new divorce law? Shaw might have treated any of these alternatives well, but not so early as 1883.

II   Lords and Commons

In three subsequent plays, one of them the sentimental *Low Water,* Pinero followed up the theme which *The Rector* had introduced amost at the last: recognition of the true worth of an individual by the mate. If *The Rector* was Pinero's Othello play, then his *Lords and Commons* (1883) took the device of Portia's disguise in the trial scene of *The Merchant of Venice* and made it do duty for four acts. But the play was based more directly on one of the "moral romances" of the Swedish writer Marie Sophia Schwartz, *A Man of Rank and a Woman of the People.*[7]

Lords and Commons is by far the most novelistic of Pinero's early plays and has the most retrospective action. The all-important past is gradually revealed: an aristocrat, Lord Caryl, on his wedding day years before had learned that his wife was illegitimate. Out of aristocratic pride, he had repudiated her, refusing to mingle his noble blood with her common blood. In the intervening years, the woman has nursed hatred of English institutions; and, while living in America, she has become a thorough democrat—an unromantic liberal-minded "new woman," with an independent fortune. At the opening of the play, she has returned to England ready for revenge on her husband and his proud family. Calling herself Mrs. Devenish, she has bought the Caryls' estate, on which are mines unworked because the owners have lacked technical knowledge, initiative, and money. With her, she has brought another transplanted Britisher, Tom Jervoise, who eight years before had forsworn the gentlemanly fooleries of Piccadilly for honest independence in California, where he has learned all about mining and has adopted American "know-how" and methods of disciplining work crews. As foreman, he will make the mines produce richly.

Confronted with his own wife in Act One, Lord Caryl does not recognize her; no Portia-like disguise is necessary, because of the changes which suffering has brought to her face. By degrees, he comes to respect, then love her; and, when it develops that Tom Jervoise's American methods do not suit the British laborers, he accepts her offer of the foremanship, after a great inward struggle, and begins to look forward to a new life in honest toil. His change of character moves Mrs. Devenish to give up her revenge and return his love. By the final curtain the nobleman is brought to recognize this admirable woman, whom he loves, as his base-born, cast-off wife.

Peopling this full and interesting plot are many other characters, some of them richly realized, who give the play a distinctly English flavor. The Countess of Caryl, whose rigidity is partly the reason for her son's, is at first a caricature who later turns into a human being; but her change is not altogether credible. Her brother, Lord Percy Lewiscourt, is a modern cousin to Restoration fops. Representing false nobility in its baser aspects, he remains insidiously stiff-backed in his behavior; and the extremity of his pride is symbolically manifest in his finical hypochondria and debility. As Pinero's first portrait of an American, Miss Maplebeck has a "humour," the impulse to be a "tease." She frequently makes Sir Percy look ridiculous; and, when he proposes marriage because his valet has left him and he needs a nurse, she refuses him. Pert and outspoken, she reads *Punch* and the satirical weeklies but scorns *The Times*. At the end, she departs to marry her loving Senator Kneebone back in Washington. Another character, Tom Jervoise, undergoes a comic change. Dressed as the "very picture of a Californian" in Act One, he falls in love with Lady Nell, Lord Caryl's charming sister; and before long, in order to please her, he begins awkwardly to resume the sartorial habits of a British gentleman and to forego using American slang. At play's end, they too are headed for the altar. In addition, there are more broadly drawn "low" characters, including an amusing old retainer.

The plotting and the character drawing support the theme that pride (of birth, especially) ought to give way to love of worth. The aristocrats and the democrats are led through changes of character to demonstrate this idea. But Archer assumed that Pinero merely intended to show the shattering of the aristocrats' self-worship, commending the exaggeration in their portraits as necessary to this effect, and called the play Pinero's strongest up to 1885.[8]

III   The Ironmaster

Pinero next studied, in *The Ironmaster* (1884), the marriage problems of an aristocratic Frenchwoman who learns to appreciate her commoner-husband's true worth. In this adaptation of Georges Ohnet's novel *Le Maître de Forges* (1882) or its successful adaptation for the French stage (1883),[9] he made no attempt to transpose it to an English setting.

The exposition comes swiftly so that the action seems to move rapidly from the first. In Act One, Claire de Beaulieu, daughter of an impoverished aristocratic family, learns that she has been conveniently forgotten by the Duke of Bligny, whom she loves, and that he has become engaged to Athenaïs Moulinet, daughter of a crass *nouveau riche*. Aware that the Ironmaster, Philippe Derblay, loves her, she manages to repress her heartbreak before her rival and impulsively but calmly introduces Philippe as her fiancé. She is motivated by pride, pique, and desire for revenge—the aristocratic emotions.

The three succeeding acts trace her problems in adjusting to this man whom she thinks so much beneath her. In the colorful second act, after a midnight ceremony in a dark church, the newlyweds are left alone in their castle by friends and well-wishers. Claire, now pondering her earlier impulsive action, considers suicide but rejects it as a disgrace to her family. Her husband guesses the reason for her evident revulsion and, reconciled to being strangers within the same walls, insists that, if she ever changes in her feelings toward him, he will remain as a stone to her. Up to this time this commoner has been entirely noble in his behavior; now he seems to have assumed some of Claire's unbending pride.

Act Three, depicting Claire's birthday celebration some months later, rises to a confrontation between Claire and Athenaïs, her old school friend, now the Duchess of Bligny. The Duchess has been alienating Philippe's affections, and Claire has tormentedly borne the flattering attentions of the Duke. She has begun to feel tenderness for Philippe through watching him suffer. At length, to avoid scandal, she must forbid Athenaïs her house; and, when Philippe supports her, the Duke challenges him to a duel. In Act Four, Scene One, Philippe prepares to defend his wife in the nobleman's way; and in a sketchy, unprepared-for second scene, Claire appropriately intercepts with her body the bullet fired at him. After a reconciliation between husband and wife, Pinero let it be known that the wound was superficial and drew the curtain, obviously reluctant to prolong these melodramatic moments.

Two characters, Philippe's sister and Claire's brother, enact the events of a romantic subplot, with an almost untroubled courtship and marriage as the outcome. Pinero stuck in some by now customary rustics, perhaps to satisfy the requirements of the company at the St. James's Theatre. The character who seems most Pineroesque is M. Moulinet, the buffoonish social climber, who laments at one point, "Bah! with all our revolutions we shall never get our backs straight as these people's"; but he evolves into a more human character in Act Four. The two scenes in which Athenaïs and Claire exchange spite contain Pinero's least flattering portrayal of women's behavior to each other.

These three plays—*The Rector, Lords and Commons,* and *The*

Ironmaster—represent Pinero's rudimentary studies of domestic problems. Whereas it was much more customary in the early 1880s (as in his own earlier plays) to deal with the woman's selection of a mate, here, as in *The Money-Spinner*, he dealt with problems that arise after marriage; and in each case he brought the action to a happy conclusion. Obviously the ending could not be the conventional trek to the altar, but in 1884 Pinero had nothing very original to offer in its place.

IV   The Profligate—*His First True Problem Play*

By 1887, Pinero was more willing and able to be independent of conventions. Having seemingly found his forte in farce, he might have settled into a routine of producing two such plays every season, which would have assured financial security, popular reception, and even wide renown. But his previous restless experimentation foretold his unwillingness to do so, and he must have known that audiences could not be pleased indefinitely by the rather simple farcical scheme. Now he gave up comic relief and the conventional happy ending (but not soliloquies and asides) and aimed at fuller fidelity to contemporary life. Perhaps he also intended to try to close the gap between the novel and the drama. Evidently not composing for a specific company of actors or for any particular theater, he asserted artistic independence by writing his first tragedy, one which continues the study of individual worth.

Though the resulting play, *The Profligate*, was completed in 1887, it was not produced until 1889; and even then its ending had to be changed.[10] Bold for its own day, it attacked the Victorian double standard and developed the thesis that a woman has a right to expect her prospective husband to be as pure as he expects her to be. To an age which does not debate such questions, it has less ephemeral validity as a study of lost innocence—both the hero's and the heroine's.

The intended tragic hero is the title character, Dunstan Renshaw, a man in his thirties who has determined to bury his philandering past by marrying Leslie Brudenell, an innocent schoolgirl of nineteen. The inscription to the play and events of the first act forewarn of his failure to escape the past. Act One takes place in the office of Leslie's guardian, a solicitor, on the wedding day. To the office come the wedding party and, separately, Lord Dangars, a divorcé and unregenerate philanderer; and Janet Preece, a country girl who had been seduced by Renshaw when he was using an assumed name. By awkward use of coincidence Pinero worked these oddly assorted figures into the beginning of a three-stranded plot detailing the outcome of the marriage of Leslie and Renshaw, the doomed romance between Leslie's brother and Janet Preece, and Lord Dangars's only temporary disgrace. The solicitor's high-minded clerk, Hugh Murray, attempts to stop the wedding when he learns Renshaw's true character; he objects to the match both on principle and out of secret love for the girl, but he only succeeds in withdrawing as best man. Later, he warns the new husband to expect awful consequences from his deceitfulness and profligacy.

Act Two depicts the almost idyllic honeymoon of the pair in an Italian villa near Florence. They are coincidentally interrupted first by some English tourists, Mrs. Stonehay and her daughter Irene, who happens to be a schoolfriend of Leslie's; by Murray, who comes from England purposelessly, it seems, unless to be Renshaw's confidant briefly; and then by Janet Preece, now a servant of the Stonehays. In an important conversation with Irene, Leslie reveals her belief in her husband's goodness and her moral outrage on hearing that Irene, knowing of Lord Dangars's profligacy, is being pushed by her callous mother into a marriage with him. Renshaw confides to Murray his anguish at knowing that his wife thinks him good and speaks of his recent charities to the peasants as expenditures to buy her good opinion. He grows in stature to the extent that he has acquired a longing for lost innocence. The revelation of his past, however, is delayed until the next act.

Act Three contains a genuinely effective sensation scene. After four days of recovering from brain fever, Janet, still not knowing who Leslie's husband is, is about to go away, even though Leslie's brother Wilfrid has fallen in love with her. Janet explains in confidence to Leslie that she has been "one of the tempted and not one of the strong"; and Leslie plans to help her away, knowing that the romance can never be allowed to develop. In a moment fraught with dramatic irony, Janet sees Renshaw returning with Dangars and cries out, ambiguously, "It's the man—the man!" When Leslie, thinking that Dangars is being accused, proudly forbids him to enter the house, Janet must undeceive her. The husband fails to deny the accusation, and the unfortunate wife bids him, "Go!"

The ostensible problem reaches a very tame solution in Act Four, but the more universal meaning comes across with some tragic power. The technique falls off notably, in awkward entrances and exits, forced soliloquies, and a sudden change on Leslie's part. Back in England now, in Hugh Murray's lodgings, Leslie wants to return to her schoolgirl world; and Wilfrid pines over the loss of Janet. Sentimentality surrounds Janet's exit to Australia and disturbs the heretofore objective tone. Renshaw, ill and worn, enters while Leslie is out of the room and indicates to Murray that his hope of reconciliation is fading. Murray abandons his highly moral stance and goes to advise Leslie to relent. Unaware that Leslie is near and convinced of her unforgivingness, the repentant profligate takes poison just seconds before the wife comes to forgive him. Since Leslie has earlier overheard Murray declare his love for her to Wilfrid, it can be asumed that she will now consider marrying him; but Pinero does not insist on this possibility.

The separate strands of the plot give three variations on the theme of the double standard: Dangars merely undergoes a period of social inactivity for his indiscretions; Janet becomes forever after a pariah; and Renshaw tries to break the pattern represented by Dangars. The cause of his tragedy is not simply that his past catches up with him but that, when it does, he, unlike Dangars, has developed a conscience. Not his deeds, not society, not even Leslie's refusal to forgive (because she arrives intending to forgive him), but his assumption that his loss of innocence cannot be forgiven by an innocent girl causes him to forfeit needlessly a potentially admirable life. Ironically, the rigid Leslie has come to take a more understanding and flexible view of his "evil"—some of the Victorian innocence has also fallen away from her.

When the play was produced at John Hare's new Garrick Theatre, Hare insisted that the ending be altered, probably thinking a tragedy inauspicious for opening the theater. The variant ending, printed with the original one in the published play, shows the hero on the point of drinking from a phial when he decides not to add suicide to his sins and dashes it from his lips. When Leslie promptly enters and forgives him, they anticipate a new life together. Clearly, the original ending grows more logically from the antecedent action; it provides the catastrophe and preserves the tragic tone. However, neither ending seems inevitable since, in the last act, the characters seem to be peculiarly free to do and say whatever brings the maximum amount of excitement. The character drawing falls somewhat short of tragic complexity. Both Renshaw's change and Leslie's acceptance of his past, occurring between the acts or offstage, are revealed, not dramatized. Hugh Murray, the *raisonneur*, registers a rigidly upright reaction to the double standard and in several sententious speeches echoes the idea of the inscription. His prophecy of Renshaw's remorse proves correct. His outspokenness and ethical values are attributed to his being a Scotsman and to his having had rigid training. Finally, however, he cannot prevent the tragedy even by sacrificing some ideals to expediency. Both Dangars and Mrs. Stonehay insidiously reduce questions of morality to their purely social aspects. In Wilfrid alone there are comical touches; he is boyishly naive and has pleasant chatter, at least in the first two acts. Janet is by no means a rustic, though she is identified with the country.

Granted that the play aims at demonstrating the interrelatedness of human actions, of past and present, it still suffers from far too obvious use of coincidences; and the soliloquies and asides seem grossly out of keeping with the verisimilitude achieved in the first two acts. But there are some fine things in it. Act One affords a convincing look at a fresh, innocent girl who is flighty and nervous on her wedding day; Act Two opens with a commendable air of naturalness and ends movingly, with Leslie's and Dunstan's parting—a parting that quite successfully creates suspense leading to Act Three; and the big scene of Act Three (Leslie's ironic false discovery of "the man") was called one of the most exciting of its day.

One critic showed how obviously he had missed Pinero's point when he called the title character terribly depraved.[11] Another, George Moore, said that he would have respected Pinero's sincerity more if Renshaw had been allowed to remain a profligate. Then, he said, he could have called the play the finest in English drama since Sheridan.[12]

V *Critical Acclaim for* The Second Mrs. Tanqueray

In the five years that separated the composition of *The Profligate* and the completion of the next play in the same manner,

Pinero overcame all difficulties with method which mar the earlier
tentative effort. He worked deliberately for over a year to write
The Second Mrs. Tanqueray (1893), which crowned all his early
strivings. A few later plays may surpass it in naturalness of dialogue or in realistic settings; but none creates a stronger sense of
inevitability or goes beyond its portrayal of a *déclassée* woman
whose decisions and character, not merely society's strictures, lead
to her catastrophe.

Like *The Profligate, The Second Mrs. Tanqueray* demonstrates
that a revealed past (equated with sexual misdeeds) must have a
catastrophic influence in the present on those who are high-
minded enough to wish to escape it; but it does so with more
complexity in character and less objectionable coincidence, and
from a less moralistic point of view. Its theme is more carefully
limited by a lessening of the importance of knowledge about the
past, since the woman's past is known to her prospective husband
before their wedding. In this play, character does not shift; no
optimistically simple change occurs in either of the principal characters. Thus individual character and social norms can be in sustained conflict.

It would be difficult to find a passage in modern drama that has
been praised more often or more highly than the opening of Act
One, which shows Aubrey Tanqueray's dinner party in progress
with one guest, Cayley Drummle, absent. Aubrey, the middle-
aged widower whose first wife was cold as marble, has determined to remarry, partly because his daughter wants to remain in
a convent instead of brightening his lonely life and partly because
he feels that he has missed true warmth in his first marriage. Since
he has chosen Paula Ray, the former companion of several
wealthy men, he fully expects to be snubbed by society. Attracted
by her unwillingness to be bound by a code and by her instinctual
gaiety so lacking in his first wife, he sets at nought the reactions of
people who will be scandalized; for their view does not consider
the qualities of individuals but superficially and rigidly labels
them. At the dinner party he announces his marriage plans and
his readiness to part with old friends and withdraw to the country,
where hopefully, after a trial period, he will cloak Paula with his
respectability. Then Cayley arrives, talking breezily and sarcasti-
cally of just such a misalliance, that of George Orreyed, who, he
says, has just disappeared into the social Dead Sea. This exposi-

tion, heavily tinged with dramatic irony, is masterful; and the later disappearance of the two other friends from the plot is mute testimony to Aubrey's having fallen into the same sea.

After Cayley leaves, having tried unsuccessfully to warn Aubrey of social disaster, Paula, delighting in defying Victorian propriety, comes to see Aubrey late on this eve of their wedding. In an attempt to be perfectly honest and to prevent an unknown past from ruining her happiness with Aubrey, she presents him with a written account of her past amours and offers to release him if, after reading it, he does not want to marry her the next day. Magnanimously, he throws the list into the fire without looking at it. Both decisions reflect a certain nobility in these two characters, and there is quiet power in the handling of this scene. But the scene also subtly shows that Paula, in spite of her playful coarseness, yearns for a better reputation and the sanction of such a good man: she threatens to commit suicide if ever Aubrey should stop loving her.

Alone again, Aubrey finds in his mail a letter revealing that Ellean, his daughter, has decided to leave the convent and come home. Paula, though she has already said goodnight, returns; and there is now visual suggestion of Aubrey's new inner conflict: he looks in perplexity from Ellean's letter to Paula and back. At once the audience grasps the possible complications of this coincidence and wonders about the future relations between the innocent, convent-trained girl and the tainted stepmother. What will become of the husband-father's high-mindedness when his pure daughter, image of his first wife, must be in daily contact with this unconventional woman?

The impetus to overlap life and art governed Pinero's choice of a setting for the second act, a country house in the Surrey hills, and in his calling it Highercoombe, the actual name of a house which he and his wife occupied from the summer of 1890 until the next year.[13] In this setting he made clear, with rare economy of exposition in the opening lines, the social consequences of Aubrey's marriage. He and his new wife have been "cut" by their neighbors, among them a bishop and Mrs. Cortelyon, an old friend who knew the first Mrs. Tanqueray. Paula, accustomed to gay companions in city surroundings and reduced now to the company of Aubrey and Ellean, is bored and restless; and she smarts because of her ostracism. She has grown quite jealous of Ellean's

share of Aubrey's affection; but, at the same time, she longs for
Ellean's companionship and especially for her approval because
Ellean symbolizes her own lost innocence. Paula, who wanted re-
spectability, now ardently desires the sanction of a virginal girl.

When Mrs. Cortelyon breaks her long silence and comes to call,
proving that Aubrey's friends have not completely deserted him,
Paula behaves insufferably to her, instinctively revealing her annoyance in a way that a truly well-bred woman would not have
done. In return, Mrs. Cortelyon graciously offers to take Ellean to
Paris as her companion. To Paula, more jealous and insulted than
ever, the offer looks like an attempt to get Ellean away from her
influence. In another display of bad temper, she quarrels with Aubrey over whether or not she should invite Mabel Orreyed, an
old acquaintance, to visit. Defying his wishes, she posts the letter
inviting Sir George and Lady Orreyed, in a convincingly motivated climax.

In the third act, the boorish and vapid guests, whose lives both
parallel and contrast with the Tanquerays', have been in the
house long enough for Paula to tire of them. In self-analytical
talks with Drummle, also a house-guest, she realizes that she has
outgrown Mabel's manifest coarseness. Unexpectedly, Mrs. Cortelyon and Ellean return. Because Paula has been intercepting
Aubrey's mail, Mrs. Cortelyon has had no answer to letters urgently asking Aubrey's advice. Hence she has brought her charge
home in order to get Aubrey's approval: Ellean has met Captain
Ardale, whom she thinks she loves and wants to marry. The ra-
diant girl seems to have blossomed, and now she does indeed have
affinities with Paula. Paula is almost ecstatic when Ellean reveals
the news to her before she tells Aubrey, and she begs the girl to
let her meet the man first. In a moment of Sophoclean ironic joy
just before the catastrophe, Ellean brings him; but now a morti-
fied Paula realizes that by a long-shot coincidence Ellean has
fallen in love with one of her former lovers. In subdued and mel-
ancholy tones, they ponder what to do. Even though she realizes
what Aubrey's reaction will be when Ellean's future happiness is
at stake, she insists that she must tell him; and the former lover
agrees that he must leave. Her almost compulsive desire to confess further illustrates her honesty and her essential goodness of
character.

With no lapse of time, the final act continues. Paula duly confesses, in spite of her desire not to spoil Ellean's happiness and not to lose Aubrey's love. Though Aubrey appears shaken, he offers to live abroad with her to try to redeem the future. But to Paula, the future is now only "the past entered by a different gate." Ellean, discovering the sudden unexplained disappearance of her lover, guesses that Paula caused him to go and calls her a bad woman— she has always known her true nature, she says. Since Paula's growing communion with the innocent Ellean has been cut off, she sees no hope of ever placating her. Moreover, since her attempt to begin a new life has been thwarted by recurrence of the old past and since her intentions have inevitably gone awry despite what is good in her character, Paula goes upstairs and kills herself. Ellean, messenger-like, astonishes the two men with the discovery as the curtain falls.

Paula's suicide is well motivated, considering the circumstances and her character: her inability to settle down to a "respectable" life in Act Two; her firm belief that Aubrey cannot love her if she grows ugly and old, based on her relations with men before her marriage to Aubrey; the coincidence that brings Ardale back into her life; her ironically misjudging Aubrey in assuming that she has lost his love; and the impulsiveness which she has earlier demonstrated. But Aubrey is also responsible, evidently, for the catastrophe. He has tried, on moral grounds as well as for personal reasons, to overcome the strictures of a purely social condemnation of a woman with a past. His high-mindedness, equated with a kind of bumbling idealism which does not face facts, has initiated the experiment in reclaiming Paula. Aubrey's version of Christian redemption for a Magdalene ends in failure, partly because of the coincidence of Ellean's return, partly because Ellean does not early enough learn compassion for Paula. All these motives and circumstances make the catastrophe inevitable. Questioned about the theme of the play Pinero once answered that it demonstrated that people are as often punished for their good as for their bad deeds, and this interpretation does indeed fit the facts.[14]

Pinero's portrayal of these two major characters has a great deal of psychological validity, but Cayley Drummle is his most artistic creation in this play. His charming and witty vignette of the icy first Mrs. Tanqueray, his flippancy in describing how he has just consoled the elder Lady Orreyed over a pancake and a cutlet, and his soberer cautionary comments to Aubrey reveal him as a man

of the world—the best in a long line of Pinero's sophisticated gentlemen—and also as an attractive spokesman for the purely social
view of life. His witty dialogue, which seems at first more appropriate for a comedy of manners than for a domestic tragedy, creates a curiously ironic detachment. Evidently this aspect of the
diction caused ambiguity for the first audiences and for later
critics. The points of view of Drummle and of Aubrey balance
nicely—far better than those of Dangars and Renshaw in *The
Profligate*. Thus those who held Drummle's views considered Pinero a conservative defender of society's status quo; those who
could appreciate the ethical implications detected an indictment
of society's callousness.

   In actuality, Drummle's attempts to advise Aubrey, to cheer up
Paula, and to take Ellean out of their domestic life (by suggesting
to Mrs. Cortelyon the trip to Paris) eventually muddy the water
instead of clearing it. Though his loyalty as a friend suggests that
he does not altogether adhere to the code which he describes, his
interference indirectly leads to Ellean's meeting Ardale. The impression gained from an analysis of the whole play is not that
Drummle is always right; he may be oracularly correct in his estimate of society, but Aubrey's attempt at salvaging his happiness
through marrying and redeeming Paula is presented as commendable, as is Paula's search for a new life. The tragedy grows out of
the three varieties of rightness and the complications of chance
and circumstance. Society, represented by Drummle, is a modern
equivalent of fate; and both Aubrey and Paula mistakenly belittle
its power in their commendable efforts to act ethically. To men of
the world who live by society's values, the play is no tragedy.

   Pinero transcended the mere problem play in upholding this
ethical outlook and by going beyond the purely social aspects of
the marriage. Paula's feelings are in conflict with the institutions
that condemn her to isolation with Aubrey; but, as Shaw noted, "in
one very effective scene [when Paula sits looking into the mirror,
Act IV] the conflict is between that flaw in the woman's nature
which makes her dependent for affection wholly on the attraction
of her beauty, and the stealthy advance of age and decay to take
her beauty away from her." [15] This question is not a social one,
and the play which deals with it has "a permanent and universal
interest" which renders it independent of period and place. The
fact that the play was popular in other countries and afforded

famous actresses like Eleonora Duse and Sarah Bernhardt success
in the role of Paula gives testimony to this universality.

The successful production of *The Second Mrs. Tanqueray* was
important as a stimulus to the author's creative powers. That he
had at first sought merely a few matinee performances and an
"artistic" success for it indicates that he thought it too advanced,
too favorable to the fallen woman, too Ibsenesque, or too tragic.
When it succeeded beyond any dreams, he learned two very important things: that audiences were receptive to his outlook and
that actors and actresses were available who could portray his
most demanding roles. He said later that knowing of Mrs. Campbell's existence and talents helped him to create his next outstanding woman character, Agnes Ebbsmith.[16]

VI   The Notorious Mrs. Ebbsmith

In 1895 Pinero gave London audiences two companion pieces
dealing with the *déclassée* woman and her struggle for a better
life or reputation, one a comedy of manners, *The Benefit of the
Doubt,* and the other a tragic problem play, *The Notorious Mrs.
Ebbsmith.* This second play lacks the artistic integrity of *The Second Mrs. Tanqueray,* having a somewhat spurious final act; but it
is Pinero's most intellectual play, touching as it does on the question of disillusionment with traditional religion and views of marriage. Its heroine—a liberal, free-thinking woman like several of
Ibsen's characters—shares Aubrey Tanqueray's nobility of purpose, Paula's honesty and status as partner in an illicit relationship, and the attempted mannishness of the girls in *The Amazons.*

At the outset, graceful and economical exposition reveals that
Agnes Ebbsmith, having nursed Lucas Cleeve through a crucial
illness, is living with him in Venice as his wife. Lucas had been
"dying" of a miserable marriage. In conversation with Gertrude
Thorpe, a tourist who has befriended her, Agnes confesses that
she is not Mrs. Cleeve, though she knows that Gertrude, sister of
an Anglican rector, will feel compelled to drop her acquaintance.
Gertrude at least remains to hear Agnes recount her parents' unhappiness in marriage, her own torment in eight years of marriage, her experiences as a lecturer warning women not to fall into
the "choked-up, seething pit," and her turning to the profession of
nursing after an illness brought on by near-starvation. Now she
and Lucas remain together, as she explains, "only to help, to heal,

to console"; for each considers the marriage tie as giving the parties to it power to waste each other's life. They have planned to
write and lecture together as long as neither cares to break such
loose bonds as hold them.

But, in the first act, Lucas begins to expose his feet of clay.
Though just pronounced well again, he seems dangerously near
relapsing into nervous self-pity and womanish weakness of will.
He tells Agnes that there is something of the man in her nature;
she admits that she has often anathematized her sex, relying on a
mannish strength as her religion. She asks him to let their union
henceforward be devoid of passion, which she associates with
weakness. At such a stage of instability in their affair, a member
of Lucas's family, the Duke of St. Olpherts, arrives in Venice to
part Lucas and Agnes and to effect a reconciliation between
Lucas and his first wife.

In Act Two the sophisticated Duke, though he acknowledges
Agnes as a worthy opponent, seems assured that this dowdy
woman cannot hold Lucas long. When the Duke undeceives her
about Lucas's true nature, she acts on her growing fear that Lucas
is about to desert her and dons a stunning gown just given her by
him. In doing so, she both symbolically admits her coming to love
Lucas in the "common way" of women and also momentarily triumphs over the Duke. This acceptance of her womanhood signifies her first step toward disillusionment.

In Act Three, Agnes is recovering from a fainting spell brought
on by this violent change in her image of herself. Symbolically,
Gertrude, faithful in spite of earlier qualms, becomes her nurse,
prefiguring the ending of the play. Another of Agnes's illusions is
destroyed when Lucas, delighted that they have admitted to each
other that they are ordinary man and ordinary woman, speaks of
being freed from her "crazy" notion of urging others to undertake
free unions. When he paints their future life together, she mur-
murs that his plans sound like her old marriage repeating itself;
she envisions herself as a useless plaything, deprived of a share in
his work or in any intellectual activity. When he asks her to promise never to be "mad" again, she does; but, ironically, she implies
that, having sadly (or "madly") misjudged him, she will not be so
foolish again.

Meanwhile, the Duke has played his trump card, having arranged a meeting between Lucas and his wife, who has come

from England. The Duke has proposed that the pair make a sham reconciliation so that Lucas can resume his promising career in politics, even if it means keeping Agnes as his mistress in a suburban villa with a few discreet servants. When Agnes learns that Lucas would selfishly agree to this plan, she sinks so low in her newfound womanishness as to acquiesce. However, Gertrude rallies her to "get up out of the mud." She and her rather straitlaced brother invite this "tainted" woman to live with them in a Yorkshire rectory in order to prevent this utter degradation. Their leaving a Bible on the table triggers a passionate impulsive outburst—Agnes's bitter speech decrying the Bible as the thing which had disappointed her trust in it and had made her "mad" years before. Left alone, she throws the Bible into the stove; then, after a moment of horror-stricken reconsideration, she retrieves it, burning her hand and arm badly.

The fourth act illustrates the same impulsive vacillation in her character which is illustrated by her first throwing the Bible in the fire and then pulling it out; and Lucas vacillates also. Or perhaps Pinero strives too hard for titillating reversals. An interesting complication is the appearance of Sibyl Cleeve to enlist Agnes's help in getting Lucas back to politics; she gives another view of Lucas and of their marriage, which further opens Agnes's eyes and makes her regret wronging this unhappy woman. When Lucas next appears, he seems determined not to be reconciled with Sibyl since doing so means losing Agnes's strength; but now Agnes, in full self-knowledge, has decided to go to Yorkshire with Gertrude and Amos to think—perhaps to heal her disintegrated soul. She tells Lucas that, when she learns to pray again, she will remember him every day of her life. He replies scornfully, "Pray! . . . you! . . ." and leaves.

Certain defects are noticeable in the conduct of the action. Most critics who have objected to the play have centered their objections on the Bible-burning episode. Several, including Shaw, who thoroughly disliked the play, considered Agnes's grabbing the book out of the fire a purely theatrical effect out of keeping with her character.[17] In defense, Pinero elaborated a "soul history" for Agnes in an interview with Clayton Hamilton. He thought of Agnes as having had a childhood torn between love of her orthodox mother and pity for her revolutionary father, thus identifying the two forces struggling within her as attributable to her heredity and environment. But the play does not clearly show this cause for the heroine's struggle; there is even a speech in which she alludes to her mother's indifference. Pinero also spoke of Agnes as the most interesting woman it had ever been his privilege to watch.[18]

The ending also came in for adverse criticism. Mrs. Patrick Campbell, who created Agnes's role, said that the first three acts filled her with ecstasy but "The last act broke [her] heart." She had liked Agnes's "touch of nobility" in the earlier scenes.[19] The wavering back and forth seems unmotivated in Agnes, Lucas, and even Sibyl Cleeve; again, a stronger sense of inevitability was needed. The retreat to a rural Yorkshire rectory seems dictated more by the Romantic notion that the city is evil and the country purifying than by anything else. The ending has been received by all the commentators as indication that Agnes would be redeemed within the framework of orthodox religion after the final curtain, though there could be a certain tentativeness in her use of the phrase, "when I have learnt to pray again," as there had been irony in her earlier promising not to be "mad" again. Nathan Carb, in his dissertation on Pinero, accuses him of propagating, in an outburst of Anglicanism, the doctrine that the fallen woman can be reclaimed by the clergy, the Bible, and prayer.[20] But his critique does not altogether satisfy, since he regards the Duke as the *raisonneur* of the play and since he does not consider that Pinero might have been saying that truly compassionate Christians *ought* to set aside social considerations and reclaim those regarded as fallen in this way.

One can best discover the unifying theme by attending to the images of sickness, weakness, and healing. Doctors appear in consultation over Lucas's condition in Act One; Agnes is his nurse; Lucas has been seriously ill; Agnes becomes slightly ill (faints), recovers, burns her hand in a sort of trial by fire, and appears with it bandaged in the final act; Gertrude, herself on the point of breaking down when she remembers the death of her little son, becomes Agnes's nurse; the Duke limps from gout and much point is made of his need to be seated, even though he tries to abide by a gentleman's code of standing in the presence of a woman. The images include references to Agnes's father's belief in the "surgery of revolution" leading to healthy healing and to Agnes's dissatisfaction with the Bible because it did not heal her bruised flesh and bruised spirit. All the characters are weak, and some are actually sick. Lucas has come to some knowledge of his need for the healing strength which Agnes seems to have; but in the course of the play this strength deserts her, through her progressive disillusionment. As Lucas needs to draw upon a strength outside himself, so does Agnes come to need a sustaining force outside herself. True, Pinero seems to suggest that this will be orthodox religion. But, in more general terms, he may have written a homily on pride and self-knowledge; for, at the end, Agnes at least has no pretense about her; all self-deception gone, she has accepted herself as an "ordinary" weak, impulsive woman. By contrast, the Duke is sick —that is, unregenerate because he unthinkingly accepts all the shams of the social code—and does not know of his true condition.

This play is said to be the one in which Pinero first set out to imitate or compete with Ibsen. It does indeed resemble Ibsen's adult discussion or dramatization of important problems, especially in its pervasive bleak view of marriage. Agnes's "recognition" seems to be tragic in much the same way that Ibsen's Mrs. Alving's in *Ghosts* is tragic; it is fearful and pitiable to see her high views of herself slipping away. Though there are distinct echoes of Ibsen's *A Doll's House* (Nora), *The Wild Duck* (Hjalmar-Gregers), *Hedda Gabler* (the book-burning), and *Rosmersholm* (Rosmer and Rebecca West) in this play, to think that Pinero wrote it simply by putting together bits and pieces from various Ibsen plays is seriously to misjudge it. He had been doing studies of sophisticated men of the world and admirable independent women in various plays for fifteen years. However, the symbolic use of action and imagery in the Ibsen manner is a new achievement for him. Here, finally, Pinero found the particular kind of outcast woman whose story could convey a more intellectual disenchantment with social codes of his own day, one who forthrightly scorns mere respectability in service to a higher ethic. That he chose an alienated heroine who had "sinned" out of commitment to a high principle is ironic.

VII Iris

Pinero's first play of the new century, *Iris* (1901), grew from an idea which he had conceived when traveling in Italy in 1899 [21] and recreates the milieu of wealthy leisured people who, nevertheless, are not happy. Using an Italian setting for half the action, it features with some tragic effect another heroine who, through good impulses, loses her reputation, with consequent social ruin. It contains his most fully developed presentation of the psychology of a luxury-loving woman.

The playwright explains Iris Bellamy in terms of heredity and environment. She is the daughter of an indulgent father and widow of an overprotective husband. Both influences have made her a weak-willed but well-intentioned woman who must have luxury and adoration. In addition, her late unloved husband has stipulated in his will that, if she should remarry, she would lose her fortune. She feels stifled by this attempt from beyond the grave to "protect" her, especially now that she is in love with Laurence Trenwith, a sensitive young man who has nothing of his own. To marry him would mean poverty, which she lacks courage to embrace or steadfastness to endure. On the other hand, Frederick Maldonado, one of the richest men in Europe, has been passionately seeking her consent to repeated proposals. Marrying him would mean salvation from an indiscretion, perhaps, but also a repetition of her former loveless marriage. She longs for happiness with a man whom she loves; but she must meet the condition of the will, representing the respectable views of society. This familiar dilemma is modified slightly so that one man, who is a Jew, represents possessiveness and materialism and the other, who has "a wonderful ear for music and sketches cleverly in pastels," represents the would-be artist.

Act One objectifies this struggle between sentiment and prudence in Iris's maddening vacillation. Before dinner she accepts Maldonado, but after dinner she impulsively changes her mind and asks Trenwith to accompany her to Italy. Her blissful stay there is disturbed in Act Two by the loss of her fortune through her devoted lawyer's criminal mismanagement of her affairs. When Iris is poor, it seems quite logical for her to marry Trenwith, since doing so could not bring loss of fortune; but she idealistically determines at the end of Act Three to try living off a meager inheritance in order to prepare herself to become Trenwith's wife while he makes a home for her on a ranch in British Columbia. Incidentally, that this man expects to triumph in the wilderness, and does later become successful in frontier surroundings, is highly implausible. Maldonado, hovering near Iris, knows her character so well that, living up to the suggestion inherent in his name ("evil gift"), he leaves a checkbook for her use if she ever needs money; and within minutes Iris has put herself in his clutches by drawing on the account, acting on a generous, unselfish impulse to give money to a friend.

The two concluding acts show her degraded to the point of becoming Maldonado's mistress, but still hoping for Trenwith to return and marry her. On his return, however, she confesses the full extent of her downfall. Though her first misstep was taken out of love for him, he deserts her, unable to abrogate his double standard. Maldonado, having overheard their last conversation, bursts into a jealous frenzy and turns her out into the street, where presumably she will be driven to prostitution or suicide. Though she had earlier treated him shabbily, he had been willing up to now to marry her and add her to his collection of beautiful things; now he will not take Trenwith's leavings. Early hints prepare for his passionately smashing the *objets d'art* at the final curtain; and he has spoken of the characteristics of his race as being curiously blended, partly of passion and partly of prudence. His emotional nature has been so tried by Iris's vacillations that he does not seem merely villainous. He is Pinero's fullest study of male jealousy.

Attractive characters surround this trio. The single example of Croker Harrington's dogged loyalty to Iris, despite cruel gossip, proves the fallacy of an earlier statement that one can count on having four or five true friends. Iris's women admirers function mainly to point out her attractive qualities but also, by dropping her, to reinforce the motif of social ostracism for an indiscretion. No one character can be called a *raisonneur,* though one commentator considers Archibald Kane, the criminal solicitor, as spokesman for society's view.[22] Both Harrington and Kane have excellent, witty lines. Their *mots* are not excrescences; they seem natural and integral to these sophisticated characters. If any speech begins to border on metaphorical richness or decoration, another character reacts with some such comment as "You are too sententious."

The plot, because its twists and turns grow out of the motivations of these believable characters, attains a stronger air of inevitability than did that of *The Notorious Mrs. Ebbsmith.* The effect of naturalness increases by reason of simplicity in plotting (gone are the annoying subplots following the rule of three) and the novelistic aspects of the play. It covers several years, in the course of which several characters drop out; and in both Act One and Act Three the lowering of the curtain signifies passage of time within the same setting. One very noticeable instance of naturalness and economy of means occurs in the fourth act when Maldonado, surrendering his latchkey at Iris's request, drops it into one of several vases on the mantel; then, having found pieces of a note arranging a meeting with Trenwith, he shakes the vases one by on until he retrieves the key. Thus the audience realizes his intention to eavesdrop and is prepared for the dramatic irony of Act Five, without recourse to the old-fashioned aside.

On the whole, the plot is very satisfying. Yet Archer thought that a *scène à faire* had been omitted between Act Three and Act Four, a scene showing Iris confronting Maldonado when she finally comes into his power.[23] The rather indeterminate ending is not inconclusive; it additionally indicates that the interest of the play lies in Iris's character and in her steps toward degradation and not primarily in what happens to her. Hamilton considered *Iris* one of the best plays of the first quarter century, despite its first presentation being somewhat of a failure.[24]

VIII   His House in Order

In the next three problem plays, all resting on a high plateau of achievement, Pinero used domestic situations within Edwardian households for a more outspoken criticism of smugness and hypocrisy in upper-middle-class British life. They continue the playwright's newfound simplicity of plot and are among his very best works. Of these plays, *His House in Order* (1906) might have been called *The Second Mrs. Jesson,* in acknowledgment of the prominence of Nina, new wife of the widower Filmer Jesson; but the title which it bears also has appropriateness. The heroine is another version of the woman who outrages propriety, but here she salvages her life through rebelling.

In the clever exposition which opens the play, a newspaper reporter asks the necessary revealing questions about the Jessons and the occasion, the dedication of a public park in a provincial town to the memory of the first Mrs. Jesson. On the eve of the ceremony, Filmer reveals to his brother Hilary his disappointment in his new wife. Nina, irrepressible in her enjoyment of life, evidently cannot keep his house in order as the late Annabelle did; and, as a result, Geraldine Ridgeley, Annabelle's sister, has been acting as housekeeper. Present for the dedication also are Sir Daniel and Lady Ridgeley, her parents; her brother, Pryce; and Major Maurewarde, an old friend of the Jessons. The titled Ridgeleys, caricatured as uniformly prudish and self-righteous, seem bent on forcing Nina to conform to the sainted image of their beloved Annabelle. Filmer, by acquiescing in this design, alarms Hilary, a diplomat home on leave who recognizes Nina's good qualities and her restiveness under this cold regime. Through the first two acts, the diplomat uses all his charm and skill to bring about a domestic readjustment; but he fails to tame Nina or to mollify the Ridgeleys until circumstances give him the power to do so.

By the end of Act Two, Nina has risen to an emphatic refusal to go to the park for its dedication—the utmost in willful rudeness, from the Ridgeleys' and Filmer's point of view; but her rebellion is justifiable from the audience's point of view since it shows her change from pliant, spineless girl to an independent woman. In Act Three, she comes downstairs in a bright pink dress, symbolic of her change. Within minutes she comes into possession of compromising letters written to the late paragon by Major Maurewarde, who was her lover and is indeed the father of her child. Learning of Nina's discovery, Hilary persuades her not to use it to destroy the Ridgeleys' memories of Annabelle. Where, in an ordinary "well-made" play, there would have been a climactic scene at the end of the penultimate act, Pinero guided his heroine to a completely untheatrical but nonetheless dramatic act of renunciation. Accepting Hilary's idea that they are noblest who, possessing power, decline to use it for base ends, she exits to change into dark clothing so that she can decently attend the dedicatory service.

But in Act Four, after the ceremony, the Ridgeleys' presence causes further turmoil. Geraldine insists that Nina give up her dogs, which have torn the governess's dress. Hilary, realizing that Filmer's house can be set in order only when free of the influence of these vultures, reveals the harsh truth to his brother. Exorcised of Annabelle's ghost, Filmer in a diplomatic speech echoes Hilary's earlier remarks that it is time to honor the living; and the Ridgeleys understand that they are being asked to leave. At the end, Filmer and Nina are left alone to rebuild their marriage.

In the conduct of this action not even the coincidental finding of the letters can be criticized; for the discovery grows logically out of the boy Derek's rummaging around in his new schoolroom, formerly his mother's boudoir. Pinero himself expressed satisfaction with the way in which "every hint and every clue contained in the earlier acts are followed up and rounded off." [25] Despite its naturalness, the play has excellent speeches for actors; and Hilary's gave George Alexander a chance to triumph in the kind of role which he took especial pride in, the role of "the man of forty." [26]

Hilary is the nearest approach to a true *raisonneur* in all of Pinero's plays; for he has polished language, keen insight, and fine sympathies. At first on the side of observing good manners, he comes round to defending Nina's rudeness even when his defense sets him against his own brother. But he would have failed in spite of his good offices had it not been for the finding of the letters, and his seemingly wise counsel in urging Nina not to use them goes by the board when he later decides to divulge their contents. He resembles Pinero's other such characters only superficially. Unlike them, he rallies away from his standards of good breeding and, by an act of the will, helps to preserve Nina's spirit instead of a code. Nina is in no way a "woman with a past" like Paula or Agnes, but she does have a background which accounts for her unconventional behavior. Daughter of a clergyman, she has been spoiled as his "pal," allowed to smoke and indulge her whims. Hilary appeals to her on ethical grounds for renunciation rather than on social grounds for conformity. Motivated by altruistic rather than by selfish reasons, she makes a genuinely heroic decision not to use the letters spitefully. She comes to be reasonable, in the broadest sense, rather than impulsive.

In his portrait of the Ridgeley family Pinero made a satiric, even bitter, indictment of the philistinism of a large segment of British society. Hamilton's assertion that in this play the playwright "began to hate the hypocritic British family with an almost deadly hatred and to assail it with the bitterest venom of his most sardonic satire" [27] needs to be qualified in light of the clear anti-middle-class feeling in earlier plays like *Trelawney of the "Wells"* and *A Wife without a Smile.* Carb laments the lightness of the Ridgeleys' punishment as if it were a blemish on the play,[28] but

Pinero never wrote a melodrama and did not evince a belief in poetic justice in any other manner.

Carb also maintains that the plot illustrates Pinero's double doctrines of compromise (by the wayward Nina) and concealment.[29] It is impossible to agree unless one overlooks Hilary's compromise with his own sense of good breeding and Filmer's compromise, which is greater by far than Nina's. Furthermore, to accept this contention one must assume that Pinero would have thought it better for the letters to remain hidden. But the action in this play, as well as in other plays, leads to disclosure and shattering of illusions, with eventual positive results. Beside the important implications of this pattern and of Nina's triumph, the themes usually singled out for notice—the husband's difficulty in seeing the second wife's virtues when he has a false ideal of the first, the claim of the living over the dead, and the beauty of reconciliation—seem distinctly secondary.[30]

His House in Order was Pinero's greatest financial success, bringing him over £50,000; and it was also Alexander's greatest success in his twenty-five years as a theater manager.[31] Archer, in a review written soon after the opening, called it Pinero's masterwork.[32]

IX   The Thunderbolt

Choosing a provincial setting once again, Pinero next wrote a highly praised ironic comedy, *The Thunderbolt* (1908), which presented a devastating picture of the greed and pettiness of members of a large provincial family, the thoroughly middle-class Mortimores. Yet Pinero asserted that he liked these characters.[33]

His background in law served him well here, for basically the play concerns a lost will and those who stand to gain by its not being found. Two lawyers figure prominently, as an objective chorus. Early in the play the questions of a young solicitor new to the case provide exposition. The answers of the family establish that Edward Mortimore, wealthy Midlands brewer, has just died seemingly intestate; that he left an illegitimate daughter, Helen Thornhill, unprovided for; that the other Mortimores—Stephen, James, Thaddeus, and Rose Mortimore Ponting—have only recently learned of Helen's existence; and that they are troubled and resentful at her presence. The lawyers insist that all efforts be made to locate a will, though the family is eager to collect the legacy, which would revert to it in the absence of a will. Helen, not so materialistic and grasping, expresses disappointment that her father should not have given her a token of his deep love for her. She does not need money because she expects to be independent as an artist, and she scorns to receive anything that does not come directly from her father. In the resolution, Pinero accommodates a certain amount of heroism in Helen's behavior.

At the end of Act Two, Phyllis, wife of Thaddeus Mortimore, confesses to her husband that, on the night of Edward's death, she had found and destroyed a will made in favor of Helen, who was unknown to her at the time. The stunned Thaddeus, who is on the point of leaving for a family conference to confirm the absence of a will, can only dully repeat phrases of her confession. The third act begins in a different setting, at a point a few minutes before the conclusion of the previous act, with overlapping which enhances dramatic irony. The other Mortimores impatiently wait for Thaddeus to arrive, confident that they are about to divide a fortune. When he does, he tells them Phyllis's story as if *he* had destroyed the will. He fails to convince them; and, after badgering him mercilessly, they divine Phyllis's guilt. Hastily they set off with the lawyers for a conference at Thaddeus's house, where the action resumes in Act Four.

In Act Four, Helen comes into prominence as the triumphant, wronged heir. She behaves magnanimously, first insisting that Phyllis not be punished, which means relinquishing the fortune herself. Then she offers to share the estate with the others; and, when this is agreed, most of them icily bid her good-bye and leave dreaming of their happy future. The humane Thaddeus and Phyllis, who have refused their share but agreed to its being settled on their children, become the exceptions by expressing appreciation of Helen's lack of either vindictiveness or greed. With the slight suggestion of a future romance between Helen and George Trist, the young cleric who lives at Thaddeus's house, the play ends quietly.

Pinero's admitted fondness for the Mortimores partially determines this conclusion, but the essentially comic effect also demands that no real catastrophe occur. Edward's will was right in the intention to give Helen all the money—she deserves it—but once the Mortimores have begun lusting after their shares, it would be a catastrophe of sorts to deprive them. They are not entirely vultures; their essential humanity allows acquiescence in the unspectacular denouement. Their hypocrisy and avarice do not deserve a harsh punishment, Pinero implies, considering human weakness in general. And Pinero's reluctance to resort to melodramatic effects kept the ending ironic and all the more representative of life itself.

As another portrait of a rather large family, this play recalls Pinero's *The Cabinet Minister, Lady Bountiful,* and *The Benefit of the Doubt.* But it differs in technique, representing fully developed mastery of characterization and plot to achieve an effect of naturalness, despite the slightly caricatured Mortimore wives. Simplicity characterizes the single-track plot, with only a slight suggestion of romantic interest. Though there are no titillating big scenes, there are highly dramatic moments. Of the large number of characters, no one is central, until Helen emerges in Act Four. The Mortimore wives, except Phyllis, are stereotyped; but the farcical overtones in their portrayals, if not overdone in production, would strengthen development of the theme. Among the women only Helen and Phyllis seem to have any warmth or humanity about them. Ironically, Helen is illegitimate, devoted to artistic pursuits. True to form, she is a Pineroesque woman slightly out of favor with her middle-class peers; and, also characteristically, the playwright's and the audience's sympathies are with her in her triumph, though muted, over them. Phyllis, being daughter of a grocer, has always been considered *déclassée* by the others. Ironically again, her destruction of the will benefits the whole family; though she becomes liable to legal punishment, she receives only their scorn for her trouble. Effectively, then, the family stands for typical upper-middle-class people of middle age, concerned about reputation and financial security, as Pinero intended them to do.[34]

The diction of *The Thunderbolt* is nonliterary but excellent dramatic speech. Despite its naturalness, it has a variety gained by having characters read from newspapers, speak legal language as well as their own normal conversation, and echo each other. For instance, Phyllis's Act Two confession is repeated in the next act by Thaddeus. Later, when Helen has given Phyllis a reprieve and forgiven her, he is so numbed that he dully repeats almost everything she says in her farewell, as earlier he had repeated, out of astonishment, bits of Phyllis's confession. On the whole, the language is rich and varied, despite the characters' seeming inarticulateness, and does precisely what the plot requires.

X Mid-Channel

The third of these classically restrained plays is *Mid-Channel* (1909). Far from being, as one writer says, an attack on adultery,[35] it distinctly treats the double standard as a problem with tragic overtones. Again it demonstrates that a woman can make a muddle of her life even while acting on her best instincts.

Its heroine, Zoe Blundell, and her husband, Theodore, are suffering from middle-age maladjustment. Seeing that their marriage is in danger, Peter Mottram, Blundell's partner in a brokerage firm and the *raisonneur* of the piece, intervenes to try to patch it up, with little success. Zoe has been loyally busy in the cause of helping her dear Theo "get on" for fourteen years; but, now that their struggling years are past and they are quite comfortable, she is bored and, without children, has nothing to do. She keeps around her a covey of young men whom she calls her "tame robins," men whose conversation is charming and whose interests in theater, art, and music she shares. Blundell, an uncompromising philistine, becomes jealous, though there is no real reason to suspect infidelity. After one acute quarrel, Peter steps in to suggest a trip to Paris and speaks the speech which gives the play its name. In it, he rather rhetorically compares crossing the channel to getting through the middle years; and the rocky shoals in mid-channel are the dangers that a married couple must face. He holds out the hope that theirs will be a safe crossing after these shoals are behind them. But, minutes after this speech, the married pair are quarreling about where to stay and how much to spend. At the end of the act, Theo walks out, intending to sleep at his club and to effect a separation.

During the four months that are supposed to pass between the acts, both Zoe and Theodore have been trying out their separate new lives; and both have become disillusioned. Zoe has let her reputation be compromised by being seen on the Continent with Leonard Ferris, another "tame robin"; and Theodore in a sumptuous flat has been keeping a mistress. In Act Two, Peter urges a reconciliation between them; and Zoe, intending to try one, tells Ferris good-bye. Each knows of the other's loss of reputation; but

Theodore does not suspect that Zoe has gone just as far as he has.

Act Three then shows Theodore paying his paramour to get out of his life. Zoe makes the first move and comes to forgive her erring husband; but, when he hears her full confession, he cannot forgive her, obviously unwilling to admit that they are equally guilty. Here his adherence to the double standard blinds him to the ethical implications of the situation. Instead of becoming reconciled, they both quarrel again. He does offer to give her a divorce so that, if Ferris will marry her, she will not be completely disgraced.

In the meantime, Ferris, having understood Zoe's good-bye as a complete dismissal (as she intended it to be at the time), has abruptly become engaged to Ethel Pierpoint, a young friend of Zoe. In Act Four, Pinero manages an inevitable conclusion, deftly limiting Zoe's choices. Just after Ferris has been entertaining his fiancée and her mother at tea, Zoe arrives to tell him of Theodore's offer to free her. Even though Ferris offers to break his engagement, it seems impossible for her to salvage anything of her life: she will not do such a low deed as spoil Ethel's happiness. Having remarked, in a dreamlike state, on the amount of good that was in her, she hides when Blundell and Peter are heard forcing their way into Ferris's apartment. To them, Ferris swears that he is willing to take Zoe as his wife; but, when he goes to bring her to his side, he cannot find her. His servant then enters nervously and calls attention to the crowd gathered below the balcony. Zoe has committed suicide by jumping over the railing. The height of the apartment having been alluded to in dialogue and established visually by the setting (a backdrop shows the top of Albert Hall in the background), this eventuality has been prepared for. Peter's curtain line, "She told me once it would be in the *winter* time——!" echoes Zoe's earlier references to suicide.

This strong sense of inevitability, growing out of the heroine's presence in surroundings affording the opportunity of suicide coupled with the dropping away of her alternatives, is the finest effect of the plot. The whole play is a model of Realistic technique, except for the rather bald exposition of the opening conversation. The motivation of the characters is both credible and psychologically sound. The couple's decision in the past not to have children, who would have given them a common interest in middle age;

their preoccupation with financial success; Zoe's having acquired
the slang of Theo's business associates to help him—all these have
made them what they cannot now help being and account for
their disenchantment with each other. At the onset of her meno-
pause, both are understandably conscious of the effects of their
decisions and of years wasted in pursuing happiness down the
wrong road. The language of the play contributes solidly to their
characterization: Zoe's vulgarity in speech, which now disgusts
Theo, contrasts sharply with the rhetorical flourishes of Peter Mottram, which likewise elicit Theo's scorn. Peter's sententiousness
emphasizes the ineffectiveness of his attempts to help the pair; in
the long run, his advice, wise as it may seem coming from such a
man of the world, cannot prevent the catastrophe.

One can find little reason to quarrel with Hamilton's warm
praise of *Mid-Channel*. He said that it treated a theme "eternally
important" to every theatergoer. Its structure, he said, was fault-
less, with no material wasted. He noted that "many passages produce a three-fold effect—first by immediate interest, second, by
reminiscence, and, third, by prophecy." He praised also the thor-
oughness of Pinero's character analysis, the "steady gathering of
intense internal conflict," and the "crisp . . . pointed . . . nervously concise" dialogue. He thought that "no finer dramatic composition" had been written in English in the first two decades of
this century. But, offering it as favorable evidence for a discussion
of the comparative merits of Ibsen and Pinero, he called *Mid-
Channel* a greater play than either *Hedda Gabler* or *A Doll's
House*[36]—a more debatable opinion.

XI Dr. Harmer's Holidays

Pinero based his next problem play, *Dr. Harmer's Holidays*
(1931), on an idea which had occurred to him in 1892 when he
had attended the trial of three men accused of robbing and stran-
gling a doctor in an alleyway. What interested him then and until
1923–24 when he composed the play was "the problem of a respectable young doctor . . . apparently living a sober, honest and
cleanly life, who met his end in such an ignoble fashion; and I set
myself to the task of forging a chain of circumstances, intensifying
rather than diminishing the tragedy of his death, which would,
granting the premises, account naturally for that desperate, and
final, fight for breath in those lone and noisome surroundings." [37]

In justifying the doctor's presence in a disreputable section of London, Pinero posited a Jekyll-Hyde duality in his character. Respectable for eleven months of the year, Walter Harmer must then indulge his strange compulsion to live dissolutely among the corrupt and lowly while pretending to take an annual holiday. He meets his end on one of these holidays, when cutthroats attack him in the lodgings of a prostitute.

This "contrast in nine scenes" has four old-fashioned tableau scenes (pantomimes acted out before a background). Three of them show the doctor's leaving or returning to his landlady's suburban home; the fourth, the final scene of the play, is entirely motionless and reveals the doctor's body stretched out on the floor, eyes staring. Thus the murder happens between scenes. The five other scenes contrast action in Harmer's office and lodgings with his wallowing in the iniquitous quarters of a corrupt city. In creating the low-life scenes starkly and in writing episodically, Pinero ventured out of his customary style.

Two engaging moments in the play reward the student of craftsmanship and at the same time express the Pineroesque outlook on human goodness. In the first scene, the good doctor, presumably sharing professional secrets with a colleague who will relieve him for the month's vacation, describes his own compulsive slumming as if it were the behavior of a pitiable patient. He speaks of "the revulsion, the repentance, the effort on the part of the miserable wretch to cleanse himself. And then, the good resolutions, the frantic prayers at the bedside, and the conviction, as month after month slips by—the conviction that at last—at last!—the abominable appetite is dead and done for!" When details of Harmer's narration coincide with the landlady's prior description of his mysterious behavior, the other doctor begins to suspect that this is a confession; and in this way the audience learns of the hero's good intentions about and his remorse over his depraved conduct. As he generalizes about his own condition, this speech explicates the tragedy of all Pinero's tragic characters: "There are thousands—millions—in this terrible world who are cursed—enslaved—if not precisely in the same way, in a way that's akin to it; who, deep down in their souls, as it were, love to walk along beautiful country roads, and worship under the arches of green trees, and who are tapped on the shoulder by an unseen force and dragged off to wallow in the slime of the ditches!"

The second impressive moment comes when Harmer, having proposed impulsively to his landlady's daughter at the time of her desertion by a suitor, has come to expect a new life with her, the love of a pure woman lifting him out of his degradation. Just after he utters an exultant speech about his prospects, the former suitor returns to claim the girl. This moment of ironic joy precedes the catastrophe, the recurrence of the old pattern of the past. As in several other plays, a chance happening cancels the possibility of fulfilling good intentions. In a sense, the play deals with a universal problem: the difficulty of directing the human will to some good end.

XII   Late of Mockford's

Pinero's last play, *Late of Mockford's,* written in 1934, was left unproduced at his death in the same year and only recently came to light, when the British Museum acquired the manuscript. According to J. P. Wearing, the play "breaks fresh ground" in relation to Pinero's earlier problem plays. In it, "he concentrates on a lower stratum of society than previously, a stratum oppressed by the economic structure of England where the Chairman of the board of directors of the local factory wielded an absolute power with his ability to deny a person a job, if he so chose. It is a competent, if not an outstanding play, reminiscent of some of Galsworthy's work." [38] It is thus further evidence of Pinero's restless experimentation, even at the age of seventy-nine. Unfortunately, the text has not been available for this study.

XIII   *Contribution*

In his series of problem plays Pinero accommodated this type of play to his uses and acclimated it to England. After several tentative efforts, he ushered in the modern English drama with *The Second Mrs. Tanqueray,* altogether doing away with stereotyped characterization and old-fashioned soliloquies and asides. Thereafter he perfected his Realistic technique in plays of consistent high quality, contributing several other classics to the modern theater. To his mastery of plotting, evident in such earlier plays as *The Magistrate* and *Dandy Dick,* he added many-sided and credible character portrayals and natural dialogue, buttressing plot so strongly that even obvious contrivances were made to seem plausible. He broadened the scope of the English drama by undertaking to write Realistic tragedy and by imitating the novel's time scheme and fullness of character, probing motives with sound psychology. Parallel with the novel's development, he turned toward franker treatment of intimate domestic life.

Dealing almost exclusively with adjustment in marital affairs (*The Thunderbolt* and *Dr. Harmer's Holidays* are the exceptions), Pinero presented a bleak view of marriage and used the marriage relationship as a metaphor for an individual's restriction by the will of another or by the code of society. In *The Second Mrs. Tanqueray, Iris,* and *Mid-Channel,* he indicted society for its double standard; in *The Notorious Mrs. Ebbsmith,* he indicted the marriage tie itself.

The world of most of these plays is dominated by social conventions, but *The Thunderbolt* superadds crass materialism. The social standards are not taken as the status quo which must be defended; instead, they clash with ethical considerations, and the protagonists are caught in this struggle. Society becomes the modern equivalent of fate, and woe be unto the high-minded idealist who does not face the reality of rigid social codes and attitudes. Such a protagonist must at least lose innocence and become disillusioned; at worst, he meets a catastrophe like loss of reputation, real degradation, or suicide. In only two cases is the *raisonneur* high-minded: Hugh Murray is ineffectual, and Hilary Jesson achieves what he sets out to do, with the aid of chance. The others are more or less callous representatives of the status quo counseling socially expedient action. Their almost uniform inability to help their friends, the protagonists, suggests that Pinero did not see any easy solution to the moral dilemmas which he posed, and did not present any characters as all-wise and powerful. He was not a cynic, distrustful or skeptical of goodness in human beings; he alertly described the fallible power of "good" people in the struggle with this modern equivalent of fate. On more than one occasion he showed that people are punished as frequently for their good actions as for their bad, and that they are prevented from good actions by chance as often as by failure of the will. The "problem" thus becomes a fairly universal one.

Though Pinero had written comedies of sentiment for a sentimental age, in his problem plays he developed and adhered to a rigidly deterministic view of man's condition. He stressed the consequences of past actions and decisions instead of showing his

characters deliberating much in the present: to have allowed
them more deliberation would have implied greater freedom of
the will. He did not sentimentally expect pity for weak victims.
Often impulse rather than deliberation governs; and the action of
choosing involves vacillation, expressed in sudden reversals. The
characters who are most sympathetically drawn do not always act
from settled convictions or designs; those who unthinkingly abide
by a code are not presented very sympathetically. Chance and
circumstance enter heavily into choices, fostering some, negating
others, even operating against good intentions. Taking the problem plays as a group, one can appreciate this coherent view. Because the other genres do not admit of so clear an expression of a
philosophy, one commentator has insisted that Pinero's variety
proves his lack of a consistent philosophy.[39] He himself did not
pose as an authority on questions of economics, politics, or philosophy; he observed the social scene minutely, and his plays have
value as social history.

From reading all available criticism on Pinero, one would likely
get the impression that, until 1892, Scribe and Sardou were his
masters; that after that date he changed his style radically and
began ransacking Ibsen's plays for characters, situations, techniques, and ideas; that, had it not been for this significant contact
with the Norwegian, Pinero would not deserve even the barest
mention in theater history. True, Pinero was not unwilling to read
Ibsen's plays and learn from them; but the other assumptions are
manifestly wrong. Independent of any traceable influence, he
began employing the scheme of the domestic problem play as
early as 1883 in *The Rector*. In *The Profligate* he made a remarkable advance down the same path, establishing patterns on his
own that were compatible with and easily adaptable to the new
influence making itself felt around 1890. By that time, he was already as accomplished a craftsman in his own right as was Ibsen.
Any borrowing that he may have done beyond this point he made
completely his own.

CHAPTER 7

Enduring Artist

PINERO, the Realist, effaced his own personality from his works and seldom commented on them or on his dramatic theory. Among his sparse critical utterances, one brief speech, "The Modern British Drama," delivered to the Royal Academy at a dinner in 1895, holds the key to his esthetics; and three other pieces, his studies of Stevenson and Browning as dramatists and his Foreword to *Two Plays*, supplement it. His theory of art grew out of his acquaintance with the broadly popular theater of the nineteenth century, but it accommodated development of a new form in that theater.

I *His Theory of Dramatic Art*

Recognizing the desire of predominantly middle-class audiences to see themselves and their values reflected in plays, Pinero evolved a theory of playwriting to satisfy this "intellectual and spiritual" need, as he called it. In some other age, he acknowledged, this need might not prevail, and his form would not be right. He posited a moral function for the playwright and thought that, in his own age, his finest task was to give "back to the multitude their own conceptions illuminated, enlarged, and, if needful, purged, perfected, transfigured." "Multitude" implies the broadly constituted late-Victorian audiences, including aristocrats and commoners; but, as Pinero's practice shows, he did not mean merely to defend the idols of the tribe. The words "illuminated, enlarged" imply the heightening of effect which is necessary even in the most Realistic plays. The significant phrase "purged, perfected, transfigured" shows that by 1895 Pinero had embraced the moral aim—a "modernist" one—of exposing the souls of playgoers, leading them to self-evaluation and bringing them, in Shaw's later words, to a "conviction of sin." Unlike Shaw, Pinero did not characteristically polemicize or propagandize; he was content to "give back." Shaw spoke scornfully of *belles-lettres* and addressed his plays to a pit of philosophers; Pinero called what he practiced "Dramatic Art" and aimed at a much more inclusive public.

Granted that Pinero wanted to interest a great number of people and, in a sense, to provide what was demanded, he thought that the drama ought to be as artistic as possible. It had legitimate ways of arousing interest that were distinct from those of the novel. In this connection, in his essay on Robert Louis Stevenson, he made a distinction between *dramatic* and *theatrical* talent. The first, as he defined it, is a general ability to "project characters, and to cause them to tell an interesting story" in dialogue. It is the raw material of the second, which is a talent for making the characters "not only tell a story by means of dialogue, but tell it in such skillfully-devised form and order as shall, within the limits of an ordinary theatrical representation, give rise to the greatest possible amount of that peculiar kind of emotional effect, the production of which is the one great function of the theatre."

Pinero also distinguished between the two parts of technique, *strategy* and *tactics*. The first is the more general laying out of the story; the second is "the art of getting . . . characters on and off the stage, of conveying information to the audience. . . ." The strategy employed by the dramatist is to some extent shared with the novelist, but the tactics belong to the art of the theater alone. Attacking Stevenson for thinking that tactics necessarily falsify life, he defined the modern dramatist's problem as "nothing else than to achieve the *compression* of life which the stage undoubtedly demands *without* falsification. . . . It is the height of the author's art, according to the old maxim, that the ordinary spectator should never be clearly conscious of the skill and travail that have gone to the making of the finished product." He knew well that contrivance was a necessity and that, like acting, the playwright's art could imitate but not reproduce life.

He further elaborated his version of the Realist's credo in specifying that the ideal play should be "closely observant in its portrayal of character," but he turned away from extreme Naturalistic effects by stipulating that it be "stirring in its development" and "dignified in expression." On the whole, it should convince the spectator (presumably through settings as well) that the events are not beyond his possible experience of life.

II   *His Practice*

This theory effectively accounts for Pinero's practice in all the genres. As a strategist, he always tried to give his plots stirring development. He recognized his audiences' preoccupation with reputation and with the mating game, and he therefore made these the cornerstones of many plays. The climaxes in *The Notorious Mrs. Ebbsmith, The Benefit of the Doubt,* and *The Gay Lord Quex* were so strong that the plays could be identified for a time by reference to the Bible-burning scene, the listening scene, and the bedroom scene. He relied heavily on the reversal (peripety) to stir spectators, not always one major reversal but often a series of smaller ones. In his best plays, these reversals grow out of and express the characters' oppressive inner struggles and establish the logic of events. Like Ibsen, he transcended the scheme of the "well-made" play by mastering it and then by rendering its superficialities obsolete.

Independently, Pinero worked out variations of a three-track plot scheme which did workmanlike service, hardly more, except in two plays. In *The Second Mrs. Tanqueray* and *The Notorious Mrs. Ebbsmith,* the triplicity of the stories broadens the applicability of the themes, almost allegorically repeating the frustration and unhappiness in marriage. Later, he fashioned more classically simple plots for *His House in Order, The Thunderbolt,* and *Mid-Channel;* and he used seemingly insignificant actions and objects symbolically with quiet effectiveness and economy. But many of the plays begin better than they end, giving rise to the quip that the maxim *respice finem* applies to Pinero in a new way.[1]

In tactics, Pinero gradually gained competence to produce naturalness. One can trace with delight these steps forward in Act One of *The Squire,* the opening of *The Weaker Sex, The Magistrate,* Act Two of *The Profligate,* and Act One of *Lady Bountiful.* By 1892, he was a master at arousing interest and in foreshadowing.[2] And, though he expended vast ingenuity and cleverness on exposition in his mature plays, he said, ". . . when an exposition cannot be thoroughly dramatized . . . it may best be dismissed, rapidly and even conventionally, by any not too improbable device . . ."[3] as in *Mid-Channel.*

In the service of naturalness, Pinero gradually worked away from conventional techniques, making a major contribution to

modern English drama when he discarded the old-fashioned soliloquy and aside. To maneuver his characters into place, he tacti-
cally relied on the assumption that a table was always laid in the
next room; his characters characteristically enter from a meal or
exit to consume one; and, like Chekhov's, they often "sit down to
supper" on the stage. This technique is more than a logical way of
motivating entrances and exits; for it accords with Pinero's linking
eating with frustration and disappointment of hopes, which describe the condition of man; and it occasions quiet, natural talk
and action, rather than catastrophes. His early experiments with
mistaken identity and disguise (in *The Hobby Horse* and *Lords
and Commons*) led finally to subtly elaborated presentation of
role-playing as it disguises one's instinctual life or serves a code in
such plays as *The Schoolmistress, The Amazons, The Princess and
the Butterfly,* and *Trelawney of the "Wells."*

His settings also remind spectators that it is their world which
they see behind the proscenium. A true Realist, he referred to
actual streets and areas of London; and he reflected myriad
aspects of modern life through his choice of settings. His actions
take place in a variety of locales: a gymnasium, a manicurist's
parlor, a boat-house, a photographer's studio, a boudoir in an aged
country house, a gentleman's study with a shaving closet, restau-
rants, the theater itself, and others. Some of these settings, notably
Letty's boardinghouse rooftop and Overcote Park, are tinged with
"fancy and romance," which Pinero thought had "immortal rights"
in the drama. Interior sets are always arranged with regard to
architectural logic, and in *Letty* Pinero put almost a whole apartment onto the stage. This practice necessitates detailed stage directions; and many of them call for carefully controlled lighting
effects—those of midday, late afternoon, or sunrise.

In drawing characters, Pinero followed his own dictum and was
"closely observant." He modestly attributed his success to his
"small powers of observation." [4] When he first drew characters
who were not immediately recognizable as entirely good, he was
regarded as a cynic; but he persisted in observing human nature
and in reporting what he saw. Perhaps he agreed with the French
curate in his early play *La Comète* who said, "We can learn more
from the erring than from the circumspect." He wanted to "paint
man man, whatever the issue," as Browning had wanted to do;
and he said, ". . . from the truths of life as they appear to my

eyes I have never wavered in any degree." [5] In the drama prior to his time, characters had too often shown little motivation and insufficient relation to each other. Pinero gave his characters minds of their own, and he made them listen and react to each other.

Even in forgivably repeating certain types of characters (in the process of writing fifty-seven plays), Pinero provided them with fresh differentiae. Beginning with stereotyped "low" characters, he moved to more honestly circumstantial portraits; but he retained the traditional device of personanyms, partly to avoid libel suits. One recurring type is the sophisticate, frequently identifiable as the ineffectual *raisonneur*. Another is the woman with endangered or lost reputation, often too idealistic in her outlook on the world, in her disregard for society's strictures, or in her hopes of starting a new life. His young men are mostly *roués*, his clerics are by no means stodgy or unbending, his youngsters are fresh and engaging. On the whole, he effectively presents a wide variety of characters reflecting various occupations and levels: doctors, lawyers, rectors, government officials, painters, novelists, dramatists, journalists, (one) photographer, manicurists, shop girls, and housekeepers.

As an apologist for women and as a student of their psychology, Pinero is at his best. Most of the titles indicate the prominence of women in the plays, even in *The Money-Spinner, The Squire,* and *A Cold June.* His women are usually comfort-loving and desirous of personal happiness, they seem always ready to act on impulse and to break away from rigid codes, and they frequently try to avoid hurting others. Lacking grand passions, however, they find the choice of a mate a hard one. They make their choices on the basis of money, manners, reputation, escape from boredom or middle age, or their illusions about these. Some are capable of unselfish renunciation.

Because Pinero wrote "dignified" dialogue, some have regarded it as too literary; because it contains slang and topicality, others have considered it unliterary. Neither assumption is warrantable. He sensibly realized that fine speeches alone do not make a good play: "The literature of a play I understand to be contained in the development of character and the suggestion of the unwritten portions—those which, by stimulating the imagination, suggest all that the novelist would describe. Really literary dialogue, if you must use the word, is that in which the right word always appears in its right place, and conveys its exact meaning with reference to the evolution of the dramatic idea." [6] By his own standard, then, much of his dialogue has a distinguished literary quality; but, when he was asked once whether he thought that his plays were literary, he replied, "Heaven forbid! More dramatic authors have died from literature than from any other cause." [7] His practice reveals that he recognized the subsidiary and integral role of diction in creating character, that it must be in keeping with the data regarding the character who speaks. He would have faulted Wilde for his excrescences of wit that are not integral to consistent character development. There is engaging wit in Pinero's plays, but it is never allowed to take on unnatural brilliance or to supersede character delineation.

III   *His Achievement*

Doomed to near oblivion in recent years, Pinero may some day receive a fair judgment of his place in English literature. By then, thorough studies of more of his contemporaries and standard histories of the period will have been written; and more of his best plays may have been brought back to theater repertories. Some sixty years after the onset of his obscurity and nearly forty years after his death, revaluation of his accomplishment seems overdue; and there are a few signs that it will be forthcoming: the appearance of some doctoral dissertations on Pinero; recent revivals of several of his plays in England, especially at the Chichester Festival; successful revival of *Trelawney of the "Wells"* in New York (1970); and reissue of Hamilton's standard four-volume collection of eight of the plays (1967). At present, only a tentative assessment of his enduring qualities may be possible.

It cannot be doubted that he did much in his time for the theater, its personnel, and its status. Building on Robertson's reforms, he cultivated a full-blown Realism beyond which none of his important contemporaries went, except perhaps Galsworthy. At the very least, this aspect of his work did away with the old unrealities of the mid-Victorian stage. For actors and managers, Pinero brought good fortune in the form of challenging and interesting roles and successful productions. Mrs. Patrick Campbell and Irene Vanbrugh had their initial acting successes in his women's roles, and John Hare and George Alexander became identified with typical Pinero parts. And Eleonora Duse and Sarah Bernhardt, the greatest actresses of the time, won acclaim as Paula Tanqueray. Pinero practically sustained the Court Theatre with his farces and the St. James's through thirty-five years and two managements; and his productions of *Sweet Lavender* at Terry's and of *The Profligate* at Hare's Garrick were landmarks, not to mention the production of *The Second Mrs. Tanqueray* at the St. James's. As one writer too slightingly put it, he "kept the theatres open." [8]

He participated in the emergence of the modern director by staging his own plays; and, in doing so, he jealously guarded the prerogatives of the author. Thus he enhanced the status of his calling. According to Hamilton, before Pinero's time audiences went to the theater to see great actors; after his time, they went to see good plays. [9]

Pinero was the leading figure in what Jones has called the Renascence of English drama after 1890; and, according to Harley Granville-Barker, he did most to make the theater of the 1890s. [10] Without Pinero's groundwork, it is doubtful that Wilde would have had a form into which he could readily pour his brilliant wit. Though audiences were ready to accept sophisticated comedies, Pinero recognized their readiness before Jones, who, also starting in the theater in the late 1870s, wrote melodramas until about 1890.

Aside from Pinero's importance in his own era, he must in the long run be recognized as having attained high artistry in a variety of genres. He unabashedly wrote pure farce, thereby purging it of the tendency to disguise itself in sentiment; and he also strengthened the old form through his genuine concern for character delineation. He cannot be outranked as a farceur by any other English writer; not even Shakespeare consistently expended on this form the care and art which went into the Court Theatre farces or achieved such thoroughly satisfying results. Separately, Pinero embraced the comedy of delicate sentiment, well before Barrie did; but he also broadened its form to admit a subtle irony. His *Trelawney of the "Wells"* will likely be revived longer than T. W. Robertson's plays, which it gently mocks. Pinero wrote sentimentalized comedies of manners before Wilde did, but he later turned to a more rarefied style which deemphasized the sentiment lingering from the eighteenth century. As a sophisticated comedist, he may be found to rank near the top. Divorcing seriousness from melodramatic sensationalism and sentimentality, Pinero pio-

neered in the form of the modern problem play, in which naturalness and objectivity made his seriousness all the more convincing.
Among the problem plays, *The Thunderbolt, Mid-Channel,* and
the perennial *The Second Mrs. Tanqueray* can be favorably compared with some of the best modern plays. Pinero was the first
Englishman to attempt modern prose tragedy—a genre which
Shaw did not undertake. Of course his critical fortune will rise
and fall, in some measure, with that of Realism, the mode to
which he committed himself.

Undoubtedly, Pinero lacked Shaw's intellectuality, Wilde's vivacity, Galsworthy's broader social concerns, and Jones's evangel-
ism in the cause of a new drama. But he also surpassed Wilde and
Jones in breadth and flexibility; and, unlike Galsworthy, he
avoided the practice of dealing with specific abuses in contemporary society—a practice which almost always guarantees obsoles-
cence as soon as the abuses are corrected. At their best, his plays
reward study and deserve to be revived; they contain near-perfect
craftsmanship of a dedicated artist, give insight into an attractive
era as social history, hold the interest of persons who are remote
from it, and express a view of life at least as sound as that of most
Realists. After reading them, one hopes that Boas's statement concerning Pinero will hold true: "Fashions change in the theatre, but
the work of a single-minded master-builder can never become
wholly obsolete." [11]

Notes and References

Chapter One

1. Wilbur Dwight Dunkel, *Sir Arthur Pinero* (Chicago, 1941), p. 7.
2. Phyllis Hartnoll, ed., *The Oxford Companion to the Theatre* (London, 1957), p. 697.
3. Dunkel, p. 9f.
4. *Ibid.*, pp. 9, 11.
5. Arthur Wing Pinero, "The Inverness Cape," *The Theatre*, II (August, 1880), 81.
6. Dunkel, pp. 10, 11, 95.
7. *Ibid.*, p. 10.
8. *Ibid.*, p. 11.
9. Pinero, in a speech to the Garrick Club in 1928; quoted in Dunkel, p. 95.
10. Dunkel, p. 14f.
11. *Ibid.*, p. 16f.
12. Pinero, "The Inverness Cape," p. 78.
13. John Parker, ed., *Who's Who in the Theatre*, 7th ed. (London, 1933), p. 1096.
14. *Ibid.*
15. Hamilton Fyfe, *Sir Arthur Pinero's Plays and Players* (London, 1930), pp. 11–13.
16. Dunkel, p. 17f.
17. Pinero, in a letter to Fyfe; quoted in Dunkel, p. 120.
18. *New York Times*, September 26, 1885, p. 5.
19. Hartnoll, p. 391.
20. Allardyce Nicoll, *A History of English Drama 1660–1900* (Cambridge, England, 1952–1959), V, 157–59.
21. "Myra Holme" was the stage name of Myra Emily Moore Hamilton, daughter of Col. Beaufoy A. Moore, widow of John Angus L. Hamilton (Parker, p. 1096). According to *Who Was Who 1897–1916*, her son, John, later became a war correspondent. Her daughter, also called Myra, later collected 365 witty sayings from Pinero's plays and published them as *The Pinero Birthday Book* (London, 1898). Dunkel,

157

p. 92, says that she later became Mrs. Claude Neville Hughes and regularly devoted time to Pinero in his declining years.

22. Dunkel, p. 27.

23. The first to do so, according to George Middleton, *These Things Are Mine* (New York, 1947), p. 217.

24. Dunkel, p. 36f.

25. Clayton Hamilton, ed., *The Social Plays of Arthur Wing Pinero* (New York, 1917–22), I, 28.

26. *Ibid.*, p. 14f.

27. Newell W. Sawyer, *The Comedy of Manners from Sheridan to Maugham* (Philadelphia, 1931), p. 90.

28. St. John Ervine, "Arthur Wing Pinero," *Dictionary of National Biography* (*1931–40*), ed. L. G. Wickham Legg (London, 1949), p. 700.

29. *Ibid.*

30. Dunkel, pp. 37, 75.

31. Fyfe, *Pinero's Plays and Players,* pp. 260–66.

32. *Ibid.*, p. 261.

33. Hamilton, I, 19.

34. Dunkel, p. 30.

35. *Ibid.*, p. 36f; Hamilton, I, 20.

36. Dunkel, p. 64. Carr already had a script in mind when he asked for Pinero's help. A study of the text suggests that the assistance was limited to creation of workable stage settings and to elaboration of a minor theme that Pinero had used before, that love is blind.

37. *Ibid.*, pp. 67, 68, 76.

38. "London Booing Pinero," *Literary Digest,* XLIV (March 16, 1912), 534.

39. George Rowell, *The Victorian Theatre, A Survey* (London, 1956), p. 148f.

40. *Ibid.*

41. Dunkel, p. 91f.

42. *Ibid.*, p. 54.

43. Fyfe, *Pinero's Plays and Players*, p. 250.

44. Dunkel, p. 67.

45. Hamilton, I, 29.

46. *Ibid.*, p. 30.

47. Ervine, p. 700.

Chapter Two

1. For an account of trends in the 1870s, see Nicoll, V, 148–53; for a list of Pinero's roles, see Parker, p. 1096; and for discussion of the "well-made" play, see Stephen Stanton, "Introduction," *Camille and Other Plays* (New York, 1957), pp. vii–xxxix.

2. Dunkel, p. 18; Nicoll, V, 524.

3. Dunkel, p. 19.

4. Nicoll, V, 524.

5. Fyfe, *Pinero's Plays and Players*, p. 16.

6. "At the Play," *The Theatre*, III (October, 1879), 164.

7. Fyfe, *Arthur Wing Pinero, Playwright: A Study* (London, 1902), p. 233.

8. Pinero, writing in "Our Symposium: Plays, Plagiarism, and Mr. Pinero," *The Theatre*, V (February, 1882), 70.

9. Dunkel, p. 19.

10. *Ibid.*, p. 23.

11. Fyfe, *Arthur Wing Pinero*, p. 217.

12. C[lement] S[cott], "Imprudence," *The Theatre*, IV (September, 1881), 175.

13. Dunkel, p. 24; Nicoll, V, 525.

14. In "Our Symposium . . . ," *The Theatre*, V (February, 1882), 70.

15. *Pinero's Plays and Players*, p. 18f.

16. Nicoll, V, 173f.

17. *Ibid.*, p. 174.

18. *Ibid.*, p. 153.

19. William Archer, *About the Theatre* (London, 1886), p. 71.

20. Cecil W. Davies, "Pinero: The Drama of Reputation," *English*, XIV (Spring, 1962), 14.

21. Martin Ellehauge, "Initial Stages in the Development of the English Problem-Play," *Englische Studien*, LXVI (March, 1932), 384f.

Chapter Three

1. "The Psychology of Farce," in *"Let's Get a Divorce" and Other Plays* (New York, 1958), vii–xx.

2. Pinero, interviewed in *New York Times*, September 26, 1885, p. 5.

3. Fyfe, *Pinero's Plays and Players*, p. 31f; Malcolm C. Salaman, "Introductory Note," *The Cabinet Minister* (London, 1892), p. v.

4. Archer, *About the Theatre*, p. 60.

5. *Ibid.*

6. Hamilton, I, 16.

7. *About the Theatre*, p. 60.

8. Dunkel, p. 30.

9. *About the Theatre*, p. 60.

10. Dunkel, p. 32.

11. Will W. Massee, "Arthur Wing Pinero," in *Living Dramatists*, ed. Oscar Herrmann (New York, 1905), p. 15.

12. Salaman, "Introductory Note to the First Edition," *Dandy Dick* (London, 1959), p. xi.

13. Denys Blakelock, "Introduction," *ibid.*, p. ix.

14. Salaman, "Introductory Note to the First Edition," p. xi.

15. Hamilton, I, 22.

16. A. E. Morgan, *Tendencies of Modern English Drama* (New York, 1924), p. 41.

17. Massee, p. 18.

18. *Arthur Wing Pinero*, p. 49.

19. Fyfe, *Pinero's Plays and Players*, p. 85f.

20. Hamilton, IV, 9.

21. *Ibid.*, p. 9f.

22. *About the Theatre*, p. 17f.

23. Nicoll, V, 176.

24. *The Life of the Drama* (New York, 1965), p. 254.

Chapter Four

1. R. Farquharson Sharp, "Mr. Pinero and Farce," *The Theatre*, XX (October, 1892), 156.

2. *About the Theatre*, p. 59.

3. Salaman, "Introductory Note to the First Edition," p. xi.

4. Dunkel, pp. 32, 36f; Hartnoll, p. 789.

5. Denzil England, "Pinero a Centenary," *The Contemporary Review*, CLXXXVII (May, 1955), 314.

6. Doris Arthur Jones, *Taking the Curtain Call; The Life and Letters of Henry Arthur Jones* (New York, 1930), p. 82.

7. Salaman, "Introduction," *Lady Bountiful* (New York, 1892), p. 7.

8. *Ibid.*

9. Nicoll, V, 179.

10. Frederick S. Boas, *From Richardson to Pinero* (London, 1936), p. 269.

11. Dunkel, p. 7.

12. As the title page of the Lord Chamberlain's script indicates.

13. Hamilton, IV, 16.

14. Hamilton, IV, 17f.

15. *Ibid.*, p. 18.

16. *Cumulated Dramatic Index* (Boston, 1965), I, 443.

Chapter Five

1. Sawyer, p. 142.

2. *Ibid.*, p. 122.

3. *Ibid.*, pp. 126–30.

4. Salaman, "Introductory Note," *The Weaker Sex* (Boston, 1894), p. 5.

5. *Ibid.*, p. 6.

6. Dunkel, p. 26.

7. Fyfe, *Pinero's Plays and Players*, p. 55.
8. Nicoll, V, 176.
9. Fyfe, *Arthur Wing Pinero*, p. 69.
10. *Ibid.*, p. 63.
11. Nicoll, V, 178.
12. Dunkel, p. 41.
13. *Ibid.*
14. *Ibid.*, p. 59.
15. Hamilton, II, 5.
16. Quoted in Archer, *Play-Making, A Manual of Craftsmanship* (New York, 1934), p. 117f.
17. As Hamilton points out, II, 6.
18. W. L. Courtney, "The Idea of Comedy and Mr. Pinero's New Play," *Fortnightly Review*, LXVII (May, 1897), 751.
19. Archer, *Play-Making*, p. 325.
20. Dunkel, p. 61.
21. Fyfe, *Pinero's Plays and Players*, p. 194.
22. Courtney, p. 756.
23. Nicoll, V, 180.
24. Boas, p. 271.
25. *Pinero's Plays and Players*, p. 205.
26. Hamilton, II, 16.
27. *Ibid.*, III, 17f.
28. *Ibid.*, p. 19.
29. *Ibid.*, p. 16.
30. Fyfe, *Pinero's Plays and Players*, p. 89.
31. Hamilton, IV, 12.
32. *Ibid.*, p. 11.
33. Dunkel, p. 87.
34. Fyfe, *Pinero's Plays and Players*, p. 304.
35. Hamilton, I, 18.
36. *Representative Plays by Henry Arthur Jones* (Boston, 1925), II, viif.

Chapter Six

1. *About the Theatre*, p. 335.
2. Miriam A. Franc, *Ibsen in England* (Boston, 1919), p. 163.
3. *About the Theatre*, p. 19.
4. Ellehauge, p. 381f.
5. "The Rector," *The Theatre*, I (May, 1883), 295.
6. *About the Theatre*, p. 59.
7. Massee, p. 8.
8. *About the Theatre*, pp. 65, 68.
9. Dunkel, p. 26.

10. Salaman, "Introductory Note," *The Profligate* (London, 1891), pp. v–vii.

11. Fyfe, *Pinero's Plays and Players*, p. 109.

12. *Impressions and Opinions* (New York, 1891), p. 190.

13. Dunkel, p. 36f.

14. Archer, "Plays and Acting of the Season," *Fortnightly Review*, LX (August, 1893), 261.

15. "The Problem Play—a Symposium," in *Shaw on Theatre*, ed. E. J. West (New York, 1958), p. 59.

16. Hamilton, I, 204.

17. Ellehauge, p. 385; Shaw, "Mr. Pinero's New Play," in *Plays and Players*, ed. A. C. Ward (London, 1952), p. 29f.

18. Hamilton, I, 199.

19. Fyfe, *Pinero's Plays and Players*, p. 165.

20. Nathan R. E. Carb, "The Social Plays of Sir Arthur Wing Pinero: An Old Answer to a New Question," unpublished dissertation (University of Pennsylvania, 1959), pp. 126–45.

21. Dunkel, p. 67.

22. Carb, p. 88.

23. *Play-Making*, p. 250f.

24. Hamilton, II, 223.

25. J. C. Trewin, "The Big Scene," *Illustrated London News*, CXXIX (August 4, 1951), 186.

26. A. E. Wilson, *Edwardian Theatre* (London, 1951), p. 85f.

27. Hamilton, III, 250.

28. Carb, p. 206.

29. *Ibid.*, p. 211f.

30. *Ibid.*

31. Dunkel, p. 75; Trewin, p. 186.

32. Quoted in Dunkel, p. 136.

33. Hamilton, IV, 22.

34. *Ibid.*, p. 23.

35. Stanton, p. ix.

36. Hamilton, IV, 281, 287.

37. Pinero, "Foreword," *Two Plays* (London, 1930), p. vi.

38. "A Pinero Revival?" *Drama*, XCIV (Autumn, 1969), 42.

39. Fyfe, *Pinero's Plays and Players*, p. 96.

Chapter Seven

1. A. B. Walkley, *Frames of Mind* (London, 1899), p. 36.

2. Archer, *Play-Making*, p. 184f.

3. *Ibid.*, p. 119.

4. Fyfe, *Pinero's Plays and Players*, p. 247.

5. Sharp, "Mr. Pinero and Literary Drama," *The Theatre,* XXII (July, 1893), 7.

6. Carb, p. 34.

7. Sharp, "Mr. Pinero and Literary Drama," p. 7.

8. P. P. Howe, *Dramatic Portraits* (New York, 1913), p. 52.

9. Hamilton, I, 9.

10. *The Eighteen-Seventies* (New York, 1929), p. ixf.

11. Boas, p. 280.

Selected Bibliography

PRIMARY SOURCES

Published Plays

Note: Titles are listed in order of composition.

Hester's Mystery. 1880. London: T. II. Lacy, 1893.
The Money-Spinner. 1880. London: T. H. Lacy, 1900.
The Squire. 1881. London: Samuel French, 1905.
The Rocket. 1883. London: Samuel French, 1905.
In Chancery. 1884(?). London: Samuel French, 1905.
The Weaker Sex. Late 1884. Boston: Walter H. Baker & Co., 1894.
The Magistrate. 1884–85. London: William Heinemann, 1892.
The Schoolmistress. Late 1885 or early 1886. London: William Heine-
    mann, 1894.
The Hobby Horse. 1886. New York: United States Book Co., 1892.
Dandy Dick. 1886. London: William Heinemann, 1959.
The Profligate. 1887. London: William Heinemann, 1891.
Sweet Lavender. 1886–88. London: William Heinemann, 1893.
The Cabinet Minister. 1889. London: William Heinemann, 1892.
Lady Bountiful. 1800–01. New York: United States Book Co., 1892.
The Times. 1891. New York: United States Book Co., 1891.
The Second Mrs. Tanqueray. 1891–92. In *The Social Plays of Arthur
    Wing Pinero,* ed. Clayton Hamilton. New York: E. P. Dutton &
    Co., 1917–22. I, 47–195.
The Amazons. 1892. London: William Heinemann, 1894.
The Notorious Mrs. Ebbsmith. 1894. In *"The New Drama,"* ed. Carl
    M. Selle. Coral Gables: University of Miami Press, 1963. Pp.
    123–89. Also in *The Social Plays,* I, 205–362.
The Benefit of the Doubt. 1895. London: William Heinemann, 1895.
The Princess and the Butterfly; or, The Fantasticks. 1896. London:
    William Heinemann, 1898.
Trelawney of the "Wells." 1897. London, etc.: Samuel French, 1936.
The Beauty Stone (libretto in collaboration with J. Comyns Carr; music
    by Arthur Sullivan). 1898. London: Chapell & Co., 1898.

The Gay Lord Quex, 1898–99. In *The Social Plays*, II, 13–219.
Iris. 1899–1901. In *The Social Plays*, II, 221–423.
Letty. 1903. In *The Social Plays*, III, 9–239.
A Wife without a Smile. 1904. London: William Heinemann, 1905.
His House in Order. 1905. In *The Social Plays*, III, 241–449.
The Thunderbolt. 1907–8. In *The Social Plays*, IV, 19–276.
Mid-Channel. 1908–9. In *The Social Plays*, IV, 277–502.
Preserving Mr. Panmure. 1910. London: William Heinemann, 1912.
The "Mind the Paint" Girl. 1911–12. London: William Heinemann, 1913.
The Widow of Wasdale Head. 1912. In *Representative One-Act Plays by British and Irish Authors*, ed. Barrett H. Clark. Boston: Little, Brown, & Co., 1921. Pp. 7–41.
Playgoers. 1912(?). In *Fifty One-Act Plays*, ed. Constance M. Martin. London: Victor Gollancz, Ltd., 1934. Pp. 233–61.
The Big Drum. 1914–15(?). Boston: Walter H. Baker & Co., 1915.
The Freaks, An Idyll of Suburbia. 1917. London: William Heinemann, 1922.
A Seat in the Park, A Warning. (?). London, etc.: Samuel French, 1922.
The Enchanted Cottage. 1919–21. Boston: Walter H. Baker & Co., 1925.
A Private Room. (?). London, etc.: Samuel French, 1928.
Dr. Harmer's Holidays. 1923–24. In *Two Plays*. London: William Heinemann, 1930. Pp. 1–109.
Child Man. 1928. In *Two Plays*. Pp. 111–245.

Unpublished Plays

Note: Manuscripts of plays before 1900 and of the play *Late of Mockford's* are to be found in the British Museum; manuscripts of those after 1900, except *Quick Work* (never performed in England), are located in the Lord Chamberlain's office, St. James's Palace, London.

Two Hundred a Year. 1870–74(?).
La Comète; or, Two Hearts. 1870–74(?).
Two Can Play at That Game. 1870–74(?).
Daisy's Escape. 1879.
Bygones. 1879.
Girls and Boys: A Nursery Tale. 1879–80.
Imprudence. 1881.
The Rector: The Story of Four Friends. 1882–83.
Lords and Commons (based on Marie Sophie Schwartz's novel, *A Man of Rank and A Woman of the People*, 1858). 1883.
Low Water. 1883.

The Ironmaster (adapted from Georges Ohnet's novel *Le Maître de Forges* or from its French stage version). 1883–84(?).
Mayfair (adapted from Victorien Sardou's play, *Maison Neuve*). 1885.
Mr. Livermore's Dream, a Lesson in Thrift. 1915.
Monica's Blue Boy (scenario for ballet-pantomime; music by Sir Frederic Cowen). 1917(?).
Quick Work: A Story of a War Marriage. 1918. London: The Chiswick Press, 1918 (prompt copies printed for private circulation).
A Cold June. 1929–31.
Late of Mockford's. 1934.

Other Works

"Foreword," *Two Plays*. London: William Heinemann, 1930. Pp. v–x.
"Introductory Note," *The Times*. London: William Heinemann, 1891. Pp. vii–x.
"The Inverness Cape," *The Theatre*, II (August, 1880), 77–84.
"The Modern British Drama," *The Theatre*, XXV (June, 1895), 346–68 (a speech to the Royal Academy).
"Robert Browning as a Dramatist," *Transactions of the Royal Society of Literature*, XXXI (1912), 255–68.
"Robert Louis Stevenson as a Dramatist." In *Papers on Playmaking*, ed. Brander Matthews. New York: Hill and Wang, 1957. Pp. 55–76.
Speech to the Garrick Club, 1928. In Dunkel, Wilbur Dwight. *Sir Arthur Pinero*. Chicago: University of Chicago Press, 1941. Pp. 94–96.
"The Theatre in the 'Seventies." In *The Eighteen-Seventies*, ed. Harley Granville-Barker. New York: The Macmillan Company, 1929. Pp. 135–63.
"The Theatre in Transition." In *Fifty Years, Memories and Contrasts*. London: Thornton Butterworth, Ltd., 1932. Pp. 70–76.
"Theatrical Byways," *The Theatre*, II (May, 1879), 234–47.

SECONDARY SOURCES

ARCHER, WILLIAM. *About the Theatre*. London: T. Fisher Unwin, 1886. Evidence of Pinero's early recognition by a leading critic.
——. *Play-Making, A Manual of Craftsmanship*. New York: Dodd, Mead and Company, 1934. Detailed discussions of various scenes in Pinero's plays.
CARB, NATHAN R. E., JR. "The Social Plays of Sir Arthur Wing Pinero: An Old Answer to a New Question." Unpublished Ph.D. dissertation, University of Pennsylvania, 1959. Repeats the casual assump-

tion that Pinero always defended the status quo; gives some critical discussion of a few lesser known plays.

DUNKEL, WILBUR DWIGHT. *Sir Arthur Pinero.* Chicago: University of Chicago Press, 1941. Mainly biographical, has little critical discussion of the plays; but collects letters, interviews, opening night reviews; is essentially right in assessing Pinero's deterministic thinking and in stressing his portrayal of women.

FYFE, HAMILTON. *Arthur Wing Pinero, Playwright: A Study.* London: Greening and Company, Ltd., 1902. Describes reception of early plays.

————. *Sir Arthur Pinero's Plays and Players.* New York: The Macmillan Company, 1930. Repeats much of the earlier book; its inaccuracies of fact corrected by Pinero in interviews with Dunkel; some important letters and biographical information.

HAMILTON, CLAYTON, ed. *The Social Plays of Sir Arthur Wing Pinero.* New York: E. P. Dutton and Company, 1917–22. Reprinted New York: AMS Press, 1967. 4 vols. Most enlightening single source of critical comment, mostly favorable; has general introduction to each of eight plays.

MINER, SYLVESTER EDMUND. "The Individual in Society: The Plays of Arthur Pinero." Unpublished Ph.D. dissertation, University of Notre Dame, 1969. A valuable recent judgment; attacks the idea that Pinero defended the status quo.

NICOLL, ALLARDYCE. *A History of English Drama 1660–1900.* Volume V. *Late Nineteenth Century Drama.* Cambridge, England: Cambridge University Press, 1959. Has a list of Pinero's plays and their productions to 1900, a perceptive chapter on Pinero, and valuable coverage of trends.

Index

169